# Minimum Viable Marketing

## Find the Right Pieces to Build Your Marketing Strategy

Brandi C. Johnson

*To my mom, who has always believed in me.*

# CONTENTS

# ABOUT THIS BOOK

When I decided to pursue a career in marketing, I went into it with the idea of helping people. I pictured myself running a non-profit or working for a company that was changing lives. Some of the companies I've worked for have, others have been more traditional businesses.

Working in corporate marketing for 15 years, I met hundreds of people who were starting their own businesses. Whether these businesses were "side hustles" or in lieu of traditional employment, most of them faced the same struggles when it came to marketing themselves:

There was never enough time in the day to juggle

all of the marketing balls they thought they needed to juggle.

Their passion for their business was getting lost in the noise of Facebook ads and SEO algorithms.

They were spending all of their time throwing marketing tactics at the wall without the focus to see what stuck.

Those challenges weren't that different from what I was facing in my corporate marketing roles either. I was focused on finding the best platforms and opportunities to drive ROI for my corporate employers.

So, I took what I was doing at my 8-5 job and started sharing it with the entrepreneurs I knew. And it *worked*. From the businesses that were selling to the Fortune 50, to the jewelry makers who were selling at weekend festivals, they all were getting better results with focused, strategic effort. They were spending less time (and less money!) for a better ROI.

You can only help so many people as a consultant or coach, and I wanted more people to reap the benefits of this marketing framework. So I distilled it into Minimum Viable Marketing. This framework helps you accomplish what those other businesses have – on your own terms and for your own industry. You'll learn how to make your own best marketing decisions today and in the future.

Before we dive into what Minimum Viable Marketing is and how it can help you get better results for your business, there are a few things you should know about this book:

It's concise. Much of the tactical information (like the user demographics of social media platforms or how to set up Google Analytics) is on the website over at MinimumViableMarketing.com. It's not in the book because it all changes, and I don't want you working from outdated information.

For the best results, register at MinimumViableMarketing.com/Resource-Library to gain access to the worksheets and spreadsheets that I reference throughout the book. They're organized by chapter so you can get the ones you need when you need them.

You don't have to build and implement a Minimum Viable Marketing strategy alone. You can join the **Minimum Viable Marketing Course** (MinimumViableMarketing.com/Course) or sign up for one-on-one coaching with me

(MinimumViableMarketing.com/Coaching).

With either option, you get personalized feedback on your strategy and implementation. Whether you're stuck in analysis paralysis or trapped on the hamster wheel of unproductive activity, you'll find the guidance and support you need to make progress.

# PART 1
## Why Minimum Viable Marketing?

# Chapter 1
## What is Minimum Viable Marketing?

How do you approach your marketing? Most business owners use one of these techniques:

1. Take a look at the competition and try to follow their lead
2. Try every technique they see – no matter what industry it's in
3. Ignore marketing and rely on the belief that the quality of their product will magnetically attract clients

I've used all three of these techniques in every combination (sometimes all within one week!) and

I'm here to tell you none of these strategies work over the long term. Even if they work for a few weeks, they're impossible to sustain.

To create a successful marketing strategy, your techniques need to be sustainable for both your brand and your personality. And that's where Minimum Viable Marketing comes in.

Minimum Viable Marketing (known as MVM from now on) is the framework to sustainably market your business. By leveraging this framework, you'll establish the foundation of your marketing plan and learn how to select and prioritize amplification channels to reach your target customers and achieve your goals.

It also helps you understand how to measure your results and design marketing tests to help you improve those results over time.

The "Minimum" in MVM doesn't mean there isn't work involved. In fact, creating and implementing an MVM strategy is likely harder than some of the other tactics you've tried (especially the one where you just pretend marketing doesn't exist). But it's a much *smarter* way to work.

You'll spend less time dissecting other people's strategies and investing in channels and promotions that don't work for you and more time building a successful business.

If you're looking for a silver bullet or magic wand, you may need to find a marketing 'guru' who will sell you a bag of magic beans. The real key to success in marketing is understanding the basics of the platforms you're using, knowing how to measure your results, and then running tests to analyze how your messages perform on those platforms. It requires curiosity, patience, and diligence, and that's exactly what this book and accompanying worksheets will help you with.

By the time you've completed this book, you'll have developed a strategy for your business, mastered measuring the results of your efforts, and learned some new techniques to increase your productivity when it comes to marketing your business.

Many entrepreneurs turn to MVM because they struggle to get all of their marketing activities done consistently. They spend hours on graphic design and social media and learning about how to target Google Ads, but never feel like they're getting the results they want.

In most cases, it's not the iceberg of "lack of

expertise" that sinks their marketing ship. Instead, it's the thousands of small holes in the hull caused by inconsistency in messaging and activity. MVM plugs those holes, allowing your marketing ship to confidently sail the seas.

## What is *(and isn't)* Marketing?

There's a lot of confusion about what marketing is (and isn't). Of course, you'd expect a governing body like the American Marketing Association (AMA) to have the best definition out there:

*"The activity, set of institutions, and processes for creating, communicating, delivering, and exchanging offerings that have value for customers, clients, partners, and society at large."* (July 2013)

Even though I've got close to two decades of marketing experience, that definition doesn't mean much to me.

Here's my definition of marketing:

*The activities you take to establish and expand your business visibility to prospective and existing customers.*

Here are some things that *are* marketing:

- Content marketing, including blogging

- Sending email newsletters
- Engaging on social media as your business
- Events such as booths, webinars, and summits
- Direct mail
- Paid Advertising, including Google AdWords and Social Media Marketing with good conversion rates

Here are some things that are *not* marketing:

- Joining 50 Facebook groups and scrolling through aimlessly, hoping that someone has a question that relates to your business you can answer.
- Getting stuck in a content creation cycle, making lead magnets nobody downloads and writing blog posts nobody reads.
- Spending hundreds or thousands of dollars on ads that don't convert.
- Signing up for courses that give the same advice you already know but claim to have made 6 figures from a single product launch.
- Creating co-marketing programs like affiliate programs or partnerships that you fail to support and then blame the partners

and affiliates for not bringing you sales.
- Building it and waiting for the customers to come.

## What is the MVM Framework?

The MVM framework consists of your Foundation and Amplification Channels. The Foundation is made up of two parts – your website and your email list. Then, we leverage two Amplification Channels to connect with new customers.

Amplification channels are third party platforms you use to reach your customers, including social media (Facebook, Instagram, Twitter), search platforms (Google, YouTube, and Pinterest), and paid advertising (PPC and display ads).

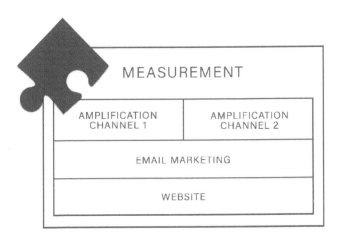

Beyond these active elements of your strategy are the metrics that we use to make sure you're continuing to grow and improve. These simple metrics will help you make good decisions on what to do next.

This may sound simple and on paper, it is. But to truly implement an MVM strategy, you're going to have to say no – *a lot*. And you're going to have to fight shiny object syndrome – *repeatedly.*

Warren Buffett said it best:

> *"The difference between successful people and very successful people is that very successful people say no to almost everything."*

## The Pareto Principle

MVM leverages the Pareto principle – also known as the 80/20 Rule – which suggests most things in life are not distributed equally. Even when you feel like you're giving your marketing your all, some of your platforms are going to get you better results than others – even if you throw lots of money or time at the under-performers.

Your MVM strategy focuses on the platforms that are driving the best results for your business. We will be giving the top performers more attention which will give you more time back to work on your business or pursue one of the other passions that fueled your desire to start your business, like spending more time with your family.

I know the idea of building a strategy is overwhelming. We procrastinate by doing mindless tasks instead of devoting energy day-in and day-out to the activities that truly move us forward.

One of my clients started a daily podcast because she wanted to try a new marketing strategy – blogging wasn't working for her but she had a message to share. One year and over 200 episodes in, she has listeners asking to *pay her* to keep supporting the podcast. Now, her podcast is the top lead generation tool for her business.

She could have quit after 10 episodes when she was only getting a handful of listeners. She could have quit after 50 episodes, or when the listener letters weren't coming in. But she stuck with it, day after day, to sustainably grow her business in a way that felt real and authentic to her.

MVM helps you confidently develop a strategy that gives you the results you want while doing work that you love.

## What Types of Businesses does MVM Work for?

MVM can work for almost any type of business, from brick and mortar stores to eCommerce, from service providers to drop-shippers and software developers. The MVM system was developed by working with all of these types of businesses and more.

If you're in charge of developing your own business plan and marketing strategy, you can put the techniques you learn in MVM to work for your business.

Here are a few examples of businesses MVM will work well for:

**Advertising-Driven:** Rather than having your customers pay for your expertise, advertisers pay to reach your customers. This started with radio and TV that were free for the consumer but supported with paid ads. It's also now common online, although more difficult to make a substantial business from an Advertising model alone.

**Affiliate Commissions:** The affiliate model is similar to the advertising model, but rather than being paid for running ads, you earn a commission when someone purchases a product based on your recommendation. Amazon Affiliates is one of the biggest and most popular affiliate programs, but many software and course providers have affiliate programs as well.

**Brick & Mortar or Retail Stores:** This traditional business model involves a retail store-front location from which you offer your products (or services). This includes restaurants, car dealerships, boutiques and more.

**eCommerce:** When you're selling your product online, you're leveraging an eCommerce model. This includes direct-to-consumer sales through your website or selling through a third-party site like Amazon or Etsy. Most businesses today offer at least some degree of an eCommerce model.

**Freemium:** In this model, you give a lower-tier version of the product for free so customers want to move up to the full or premium (a.k.a. paid version) later. It's often used in subscription-based businesses where the lifetime value is high and the cost of serving one additional customer is low. A few common examples include Spotify, Pandora, and Evernote.

**Subscriptions:** Recurring Revenue/Subscription models seem to be the holy grail of many businesses today. You sell to a customer once and they pay you indefinitely. Software providers (Software-as-a-Service/SaaS), subscription boxes, membership sites and gym memberships all fit into the realm of recurring revenue or subscription models.

**Services:** In this traditional business model, you're selling a service rather than a product. This includes offline, in-person services like hair stylers and electricians, as well as online services like Facebook Ad specialists or graphic designers. Many freelancers have a service model. Services can be priced on a per-hour or per-project basis.

MVM is a powerful marketing system that works for all kinds of businesses. In fact, I've used this framework to help businesses in one industry expand into others – like graphic designers who have moved from doing individual client projects to subscription-based services for templates and stock graphics and trainings on how to do their own basic design updates.

Building and using your MVM framework may give you the chance to do even more with your business than you dreamed possible.

# Chapter 2
## The Role Of Branding In MVM

*"A brand is the set of **expectations**, **memories**, **stories** and **relationships** that, taken together account for a consumer's decision to purchase one product or service over another."* – Seth Godin

While this isn't a comprehensive guide to branding, it's still important to understand the basics of branding before we start building your MVM strategy. Leveraging MVM makes it easier to stay on-brand because you're executing plans rather than just trying something to see how it works. You have the opportunity to create content, messaging, and graphics that reflect your brand instead of throwing together whatever you can find on your desktop.

Brand goes beyond the name of your product (like Crest or Colgate or Tom's). It also silently communicates the intangible perceptions of your product or service. It's the glue binds your MVM tactics to create cohesion.

If that sounds daunting, consider your brand as the *promise* that comes with your product or service. For example, when you buy Crest toothpaste, you expect cleaner teeth. But when you choose Crest over Colgate or Tom's or any of the other myriad of toothpaste choices available, you're also buying into the perception of "the best solution to protect and whiten my teeth and give me fresher breath."

Of course, Crest is a huge name with a multi-million-dollar marketing budget every year to position and establish the brand. So, you might be wondering why this matters when you're just starting out?

**It matters because first impressions matter.**

Whether you're working on your first sale, your 10,000<sup>th</sup> sale, or your millionth, the first impression with each customer matters. In fact, the way you manage your brand is even *more* important when you're just starting out or have a small marketing budget.

Let's look at an example of a poor first impression. A new restaurant opened up in your neighborhood so you decide to try it out. The hostess begrudgingly tears herself away from her phone at the bar to take you to a (slightly dirty) table.

Are you looking forward to recommending this place to your friends? That's an example of how your relationship with your customers reflects on your brand.

Branding is really about how you convey your promise – through your logo, color choices, the words you choose in your marketing, where you market, and how you interact with your customers throughout your relationship with them.

While there's no magic formula to ensure you're on brand, there are two key ways you can tell you're on track:

1. **When you look at all the content you put out, it looks and sounds cohesive.**

This goes beyond just the colors you use but also includes your fonts, images, and language. While different platforms can have a slightly different tone (Facebook is typically more casual than LinkedIn), you'll want your customers to recognize you across all platforms.

2. **Your audience feels the way you want them to when they interact with your content.**

Remember, we purchase from brands that make us feel a certain way – whether it's empowered or happy or understood. Does your written and visual content make them feel like staying connected to your brand is going to continue to make them feel that way?

# DEFINING YOUR BRAND EXERCISE

One way to help you understand your current brand is to find out what your customers would say about your business now. Would they describe it as friendly? Approachable? Corporate? Trustworthy? Efficient? Accurate? If you're not sure, you can always ask them.

Then, identify how you *want* people to describe your brand in 3-5 words or short phrases.

If these two lists don't match, then through the execution of your MVM strategy, you need to ensure your efforts reflect how you want your customers to talk about you.

Here's a quick example:

If I sell accounting software to business owners who do their own bookkeeping, I want people to describe my brand as trustworthy, efficient, accurate, and user-friendly.

When I survey my customers, they describe us as friendly, trustworthy, and complex.

This exercise shows that while I want my customers to see my product as simple/user-friendly, they actually see it as complex and complicated. I have an opportunity to update my training programs to help make it easier to use. I may even choose to update the software itself for the next update to simplify some processes.

## ACTION STEPS

1. Create your ideal brand definition. Write those 3-5 words or phrases that you'd like people to use to describe your business.

2. Survey your audience. The easiest way is to send an email to your existing audience with a one or two question survey. Use a survey tool (like SurveyMonkey) or a Google Form rather than just asking for them to reply, so you're more likely to get honest answers. You can use an optional incentive (like a coupon code for their next purchase or a bonus training) if they *choose* to leave their email address.

3. Compare the results of your survey with your ideal brand definition. You may find descriptions in the results that you didn't

expect but that resonate with how you want customers to perceive your brand. You'll also probably identify some areas where you can improve –through your visual branding, your messaging, or both.

BRANDI C. JOHNSON

# PART 2
# Building The Foundations of Your MVM Strategy

# CHAPTER 3
## Implementing MVM in an Established Organization

MVM isn't just a strategy for start-ups. Businesses at any stage can leverage the MVM framework to establish their marketing foundation. It's an especially valuable tool when your business is changing direction or expanding into a new product line.

Of course, if you're running an established business, you're probably wondering how to narrow down your existing platforms into just two amplification platforms and what you should do with the rest.

First, you need to understand what's actually working in your marketing and what's not. Most often we're spending time on amplification channels that have little to no impact on our business. The best way to get to this is through your business data – including Google Analytics and your CRM.

After you've identified what is working the best to grow your audience, generate qualified leads, and drive sales, then you can make better decisions about the channels that are not performing at their peak.

**Figuring Out What's Working – And What's Not**
To answer this question, you'll need to dig into a few stats from your website traffic and social media engagement. It's ok if you've been avoiding this like the plague – with the help of MVM you'll get comfortable with the basics of measuring your performance.

If you have a website with Google Analytics installed, start there. If not, we'll cover setting up Google Analytics on the companion website and in Chapter 14. It's an important part of the foundation of your MVM strategy, so don't just breeze past it because you feel like you've been doing ok without it. You should be able to find all these stats in less than 30 minutes.

**Traffic Sources:** Under Acquisition > Channels in your Google Analytics dashboard, you can see what drives traffic to your website. Identify your top 10 sources of traffic. Compare the amount of traffic that you get from those sources to the amount of work that you're putting into them. For example, if you're spending loads of time on Instagram, but you're not getting *any* traffic from it, it's probably going to end up on the cutting room floor.

**Conversions:** Conversions will tell you which pages are generating the activity for your business – including which freebies or lead magnets (like whitepapers, checklists, or coupon offers) are generating the most growth for your list. For a more detailed review, look at Goals based on Traffic Sources. This lets you see what the sources of traffic (like Pinterest) are driving the most leads or audience growth for your business.

If you're not using a lead magnet, you can dive

into the behavior flow that gets people to schedule a call or request a demo. Behavior flow shows you how people navigate through your website, including which pages they come to first and where they go after they've arrived. You can find Behavior flow under Behavior > Behavior Flow in the left-hand navigation.

**ROI (Return on Investment):** If your list of what's working is still pretty long after looking at traffic sources and conversions, it's time to review which of these leads is the most valuable. Depending on your business technology stack, you may need to get into your CRM for this or your eCommerce system.

The easiest metric to review is the channels generating the leads which resulted in the largest sales. If you have a repeat-purchase product (like specialty tea blends), you'll want to use Customer Lifetime Value rather than largest sales[i].

**Cut What's Not Working**

Now that you know what's working for your business, you've probably started to identify some things that *aren't*. For those, you have a couple of choices to make:

1. **Streamline the channel:** if you're attached to posting on Twitter but don't get great results, you can use automation tools like Later or Buffer to auto-schedule tweets for you. While it's not ideal, you can also connect platforms so they auto-post based on your RSS feeds or email campaigns. There's a list of my current favorite marketing technology tools – including social media scheduling tools – on our website minimumviablemarketing.com

2. **Pause the channel:** you can pause using that channel while you're focusing on your MVM amplification platforms. Don't just abandon the platform and leave your followers wondering what happened. If the channel has a timeline, like Facebook, Twitter, or Instagram, post and pin a message about where new followers can find you. If they're not time-based, like Pinterest, you can leave your profile open but inactive until you're ready to come back to it.

Of course, there are going to be channels that aren't driving you amazing results that you don't want to give up – like a Facebook Group or other community. You'll need to rethink the strategy and goals of that channel.

If it's a community, you can also leverage natural leaders of the community to take on small leadership roles including being a weekly ambassador or moderating the community posts. This helps spread the time investment across multiple people and can help turn your fans into super-fans and advocates of your business.

If it's a platform you just love, revisit your goals. Are you getting good engagement but no conversions? Does it serve as a place where you get ideas for new products or market offerings? Do you learn from your community? These can still serve a valuable purpose in your business but you need to be realistic about the amount of time you're spending on those channels.

# Chapter 4
## Your Two-Part MVM Foundation

*If you have built castles in the air, your work need not be lost; that is where they should be. Now put foundations under them.* - Henry David Thoreau

Most businesses start as castles in the air. We start out with an idea and before we know it, we've got a home-based goat lotion business through word of mouth and elbow grease.

No matter what stage your business is in, it's not too late to build a strong marketing foundation to support it for years to come.

The foundation of your marketing presence has two parts: a website and an email list.

These two components are important no matter what business you're in - from coaching to making handmade sweaters to installing hot water heaters. Your website is the digital home for your business, while your email list allows you to keep in touch with your customers and prospects over time. Both of these work with your brand to provide a cohesive package that you can leverage today and in the future.

Now, you may already have an amazing presence on Facebook or thousands of followers on YouTube – so why should you have a website *and* an email list?

This may not feel like the *minimum* amount of work. Remember, MVM isn't about doing the least work possible – it's about creating the strongest foundation that will get you results over the long term.

Platforms like Facebook and YouTube have a place in your MVM strategy but because of their potential for uncontrollable change (like algorithms and advertising models), they're not the best place to build your foundation.

**Why a Website?**
Window Signs. Phonebooks. Search Engines. What do they all have in common?

They're all ways that business owners have let people know about their products and services. And they've changed over time. While a brick and mortar business still may depend on window signs and displays, online businesses don't have that luxury. Nor do they have the luxury of walk-by, drop-in traffic.

Once the world got a little bigger (and more connected), companies started listing their businesses in the phonebook. The first phonebook was published in 1878. It listed 50 individuals, businesses, and other offices in New Haven, Connecticut, that had telephones. Now 140 years later, most homes and businesses don't even have a phonebook lying around.

So that brings us to search engines (like Google, Bing, or Duck Duck Go). Consumers today carry a virtual encyclopedia of information in their pockets. They can find anything and everything within seconds.

If you want to be something they find, you *need* a website – 93% of online experiences begin with a search engine and 47% of people click on one of the first three listings[ii].

Just listing your business on social media or a directory site like Yelp won't cut it. You wouldn't leave your business in the hands of a total stranger, so your web presence shouldn't depend on them either. (And no, just because you follow Mark Zuckerberg on Facebook or saw *The Social Network* that doesn't make you friends).

**Why an Email List?**
Just like you wouldn't count on your listing in a phonebook for customers to find you today, you don't want to hope that your customers remember you when they're ready to make a purchase.

That's why it's important to build an email list of customers and prospects for your MVM strategy. With an email list, you can reach your customers with new offers, new messages, and more. Plus, you can build relationships with them over time, leading to bigger purchases, easier referrals, and a higher customer lifetime value.

Around 69% of businesses spend time and money on email marketing,[iii] and it's no surprise – email is almost 40x more effective than Facebook and Twitter combined to help you convert prospects into customers.[iv] You can send product and company updates, promotional emails, newsletters, event invitations, and even ask for feedback from your customers.

Beyond just asking for feedback from your customers, you can learn a lot about them from how they respond to your messages. Email marketing systems allow you to see who's opening, and what they're clicking on at an individual level, so your email marketing can get smarter and get you even better results over time.

Are you convinced? Good, let's dig into how to build a simple website and email list as an unshakable foundation for your MVM strategy.

# Chapter 5
## Your Website

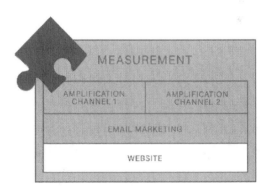

Your website doesn't have to be an expensive, complicated, or high-maintenance part of your business. In fact, you can get started with just 6 pages: the home page, a Product or Services Page, an About Page, a Contact Page, and a Privacy Policy.

Here's what you'll do in this chapter:

[__] Create a magnetic About Page
[__] Write your sellable Product or Services Page
[__] Build Contact Pages that drive connections
[__] Create a Privacy Policy that protects you and
     your customers
[__] Weigh the pros and cons of blogging
[__] Learn about the technology to protect your
     website
[__] Uncover the basics of SEO to help your
     website get found by search engines

**Website Goals**
Before you start building or revising your website (either on your own or with a web developer), it's important to have a checklist of what you'd like your website to accomplish:

- **Communicate how your business is unique**. Even if you're a plumber, there's something unique about your business. Maybe it's your customer service or your response times or your guarantee. One thing that's undeniably different about your business is YOU. What made you start this business? Why do you continue to be passionate about it?

- **Give your visitor a clear sense of what your company offers**. It may be obvious to you what you offer, but your website should make it clear to your customers what you do *and do not* offer. This is often done through a list of services but if you're cover a wide niche, you may also find it easier to list things you *don't* do.

- **Provide contact information.** It may seem like a no-brainer, but your website should include several ways to get in touch with you. This could include your phone number, physical location, email address or a contact form. Don't make it hard for your visitors to find a way to get in touch.

- **Share third-party validation.** Don't just tell customers that you're the best – *show* them by sharing testimonials from some of your biggest fans. When possible, include photos of the customers with the quotes to bring personality and humanness to the review.

- **Give clear direction on next steps.** The best websites are easy to use. Use clear calls-to-action for what you want the customer to do, easy-to-use navigation, and step-by-step instructions when needed. For example, if you only take new clients based on an application basis, let them know what to expect through that process, including how long it usually takes and the standard criteria for acceptance.

Before we started working together, one of my clients paid thousands for a custom-developed website. It had intricate menus, interactive calculators and fell flat when it came to connecting with prospective customers and building their business.

One of the first things we did was take the website back to basics using several of these tips – including optimizing their Contact Pages and re-writing the pages using their brand voice (not the voice of the agency who built the original site.) Their lead volume from the website more than doubled within 3 months.

**How to Create a Magnetic About Page**
Your About Page should provide a story that humanizes your brand - how your business got started, what inspires and motivates you, and why

you're passionate about what you do. Every business has a story to tell and this page is where you should be telling it.

Stories have been used for hundreds of years to build connections between people. It's even more important now that transactions happen even faster with technology.

So, how do you make your story compelling?

Customers relate best when they can see themselves in the story, particularly when they can identify you're solving the problem they have. And yes, even if you're selling products that feel like a splurge or luxury - like custom bath bombs or specialty dog leashes - you're still solving a customer's problem.

Here are the four key components you need to share in your business story. We'll use Carrie, the owner of a specialty dog leash company, as an example:

- **How you identified the problem.** Carrie was tired of losing her bland leashes at the dog park. Everyone's leashes looked alike - always a solid color without any real personality. Carrie and her two dogs were full of personality that her pet accessories didn't express.

- **Spark of genius: when you realized you could solve the problem.** Carrie's father was a leather smith and her grandmother was a seamstress. She decided to take the skills she had learned from them over the years and create a couple of custom leashes for her precious pooches.
- **Start solving the problem for others.** The first time she took her new leashes to the dog park, she started getting comments. By the third time, she started taking custom orders. Based on the feedback from those first few orders, she realized that more people than she knew were interested in custom leashes for their dogs too.
- **Connect your mission.** Carrie wanted to help other dog owners express their personality and love of their pets with custom and semi-custom dog leashes, collars and harnesses. She started her online store to help dog owners around the world. She also donates 10% of all of her profits back to the local dog rescue organization. In every package, she includes a picture of a pup

from the rescue her business supports.

As an established business owner, your story is even more powerful. You can include details about how many years you've been serving your customers, or how many customers you've helped achieve their goals.

Of course, there are also a few things that you *shouldn't* do with your About Page:

- **Stuff it with industry jargon**. People like and appreciate straight talk about who you are and what you do. Industry jargon doesn't make you sound smart – it often sounds aloof and unapproachable. And if someone is new and can't figure out what you do, they won't know if they need your product or service.
- **Include boring, off-brand images**. Images can communicate 1000 words so choose the images for your About Page carefully. They should align with your brand and encourage the reader to make a connection. Whether that's candid headshots of your team, photos of customers with your products, or even historical photos of your products through the ages, your About Page isn't where you want to just grab the first flat-lay

you come across.

- **Create laundry lists of bland commercial values.** Few things are as uninspiring as a bullet list of generic values that don't align with the rest of your messaging or speak to your customers. When a first-time visitor encounters them, they'll think "more corporate blah blah blah" and keep scrolling. Instead, demonstrate your values using customer-inspired stories.
- **Overshare.** There's a fine line between being engaging and oversharing, so tread carefully. When they're done reading, your visitor should be able to share what you do clearly and succinctly and understand your brand values. Remember, you're sharing a short, relatable story - not your autobiography.
- **Employ coy or clever calls to action**. Let your reader know how to continue the conversation with you – whether that's signing up for your email newsletter, writing a review, or placing another order. Don't make them think about it – make it easy for them to say *yes*.
- **Using video alone.** Video content is a great way to give your brand personality but not

everyone loves video. If someone's browsing your site at work or on the train, they may not want to watch your brand video just to figure out who in the heck you are. Be sure to include a text option for the video-averse among us.

- **Skip SEO.** Your About Page has the opportunity to be a power-house of SEO links, especially as you establish your brand. In some examples I've seen, well-crafted About Pages have generated thousands of organic page views because they were well-optimized. Plus, many of those page views turned into email subscribers and leads because the pages had appropriate calls-to-action and conversion-optimized forms.

Your customers choose to buy from you because they're connecting with and supporting a *real-life person* - not just a nameless, faceless conglomerate. Leveraging your About Page helps give your business a friendly face to purchase from again and again.

## Writing A Sellable Product or Services Page

Another key page for your business website is your Product or Services Page. This page provides more insights into how clients can work with your business. Your sales or services pages allow visitors to see what you do *and what you don't*. Your type of business will determine the format and style of your services or sales page but here are a few examples:

- Restaurant menus
- Beauty Salons and Spas have a list of services
- Plumbers, electricians, and handymen have lists of services
- Software as a Service (SaaS) companies have pricing pages – for their tiers of subscription service
- Coaches and Consultants usually have a "Work with Me" page
- Infopreneurs, like authors and course creators, have sales pages for their products

What makes these pages successful? Just like your About Page, your services or sales page needs to be focused on the customer's desired outcomes. You may be thinking *"But wait, isn't this about what* **I do**?"

Yes, it is. But it's about what you do FOR THEM. Your page should clearly answer the question, "Can this person help me solve this problem?"

(Yes, needing a haircut or a massage can be considered a problem!)

- **Make the list as complete as possible.** Your service or sales page is not a place to skimp on details. By sharing as much as possible, you pre-answer questions from your customers and start building trust. If listing everything you do is too long, focus on your most popular products or services with a short list of products and services that you don't offer.
- **Include base pricing.** Even if your packages are customized depending on the needs of the client, it helps both you and them to decide if you're the right fit for their needs. If their budget is $50 and your services start at $5000, it's not worth either of your time to schedule a consultation.
- **Focus on next steps.** Make it easy for your visitor to take the next step to work with you – to book an appointment, to order, or to schedule a consultation call. Don't make them jump through hoops. This also means including clear calls to action throughout your pages.
- **Benefits, not features, first.** As we talked about in an earlier chapter, the majority of

our purchases are emotional. We buy because of how we want to feel. (Granted, an emergency hot water heater replacement is a less emotional purchase.) So focus on the *benefits* of choosing your business and services.

- **Don't leave features out.** With the focus on benefits, it's easy to forget you need to share some of the features as well. How many modules does your course include? How many users can use the software with the licensing? Once you've appealed to the emotional side of buying, you also need to deal with the analytical and logical side that rationalizes the decision.
- **FAQs:** Depending on your type of business, you may want to include some FAQs on your sales or service page. For example, I offer marketing coaching services that have a very different set of FAQs than my online courses, so each of those pages has their own FAQs. On the other hand, most of the SaaS companies that I've consulted with have a stand-alone FAQ page that applies to their full product line.

## Contact Pages that Drive Connections

Contact pages come in second (or a close third) to the most page views on a site (with the home page leading the pack). This is especially true for service-based companies like agencies, coaches, and contractors.

Rather than just embed a standard form, invest some time in your Contact Page. After all, this is often where your one-on-one communication with a potential customer begins. Here are some best practices for your Contact Page:

- **Encourage your visitors to contact you.** Some people find contacting a stranger intimidating – even through a contact form or email address. Make your Contact Page friendly and approachable with a splash of brand personality to boot. If it's too sterile a more timid user may scurry onto a competitor's site.
- **Keep it simple.** Don't put too many barriers between your reader and the connection with you they're looking for. Keep your Contact Page short, sweet, and to the point. If you use a contact form, only ask for the essentials (name, email address, and their message). I also like to give them a quick drop-down of common reasons people get in touch (like guest blogging or podcast

appearances, interviews, course reviews, or marketing questions.)

- **If you're not open to something, say so.** Outbound prospectors and spammers alike (and yes, there is a difference) both turn to contact forms when they can't find an email address. If you're not open to messages offering you services, say so on your Contact Page. Not everyone will respect it but it can cut down on your inbox clutter.
- **Provide options.** Not everyone wants to submit a contact form that goes off into the void while they're left wondering if they're ever going to hear back. You can add other ways that visitors can get in touch with you, like social media profiles. If you have a physical location, be sure to include your address, phone number, and hours of operation.
- **Make it look good.** When users visit your Contact Page, they're beginning a relationship with you. They want to know more about you and your Contact Page design and style will be part of their initial impression. Make sure it is on-brand and accurate – not thrown together as an afterthought.

- **Consider adding FAQs.** If you read the section on Sales & Service Pages, you may be surprised to see another recommendation for FAQs. The FAQs on your Contact Page can be more specifically related to why people contact you, rather than your products and services. For example, a restaurant may address how to make reservations on their Contact Page in an FAQ section, while a blogger may want to address questions about getting their product featured on the blog.

## Legal Stuff

It's best to have a couple of legal best-practices in place. Generally, there are the two big things most websites need:

- **Privacy Policy.** If you're collecting information from your users, whether it's to subscribe to your email newsletter, request a quote, or download a sample chapter of your latest book, then you are legally required to have a Privacy Policy. There are several services that can help you generate a Privacy Policy, including freeprivacypolicy.com and TermsFeed Privacy Policy Generator[v]. You may also work directly with a lawyer to craft your Privacy Policy. Add a link to your Privacy Policy in your footer so it appears on every page of your website.

- **Terms and Conditions.** Terms and Conditions are the rules for using your website. They limit your liability if a website visitor or user decides to take you to court and protects your rights to the content of your website. Unlike the Privacy Policy, you're not legally required to have Terms & Conditions but it does help give your customers confidence in working with you. TermsFeed also offers a Terms and Conditions generator[vi], or you can work directly with a lawyer to craft a unique document for your business. Just like your Privacy Policy, you should link to your Terms and Conditions in your website footer.

Depending on your business location, there may be other legal requirements (like a statement about how your website uses tracking cookies). If you're unsure, you can check with a local small business development center or business attorney.

## To Blog or Not to Blog

Many business owners today think that having a website is synonymous with having a blog. They don't want to get caught up in writing daily or weekly, trying to come up with content and learn SEO, so they decide to avoid having a website altogether.

However, there are MILLIONS of successful business websites that don't have a blog. Whether or not you need a blog depends on the nature of your business and your ability to maintain a blog regularly. Here are the top reasons you may need a blog:

1.  Helps **differentiate you in the market.** At first glance, your business may not look much different from the competition. Blogging gives you the opportunity to share more of what makes you and your company unique and why a site visitor should choose you.

2.  **It helps promote your business.** People are more likely to share a helpful blog post than a generic company web page. You can get more organic (AKA FREE) publicity by creating relevant, helpful content.

3.  **Gives you more information about your audience.** You'll have to start creating content

before you'll be able to start seeing what content they're visiting, using and sharing the most. Once you have those metrics from your website analytics, you can create more content in those niche areas to attract more attention and traffic to your site. We'll go more in-depth with website analytics in Chapter 14: Website Metrics.

4. **Improved SEO.** Creating blog content gives you more opportunities to rank for keywords in your industry. Search engines also reward you for producing fresh content and using relevant keywords – both of which are accomplished through blogging.

5. **Content to share on social media.** If you're interested in content marketing and social media marketing, blog posts make great sharable links that aren't just a hard promotion.

6. **Give readers more.** You can get people coming back to your site more frequently if there's something new to discover. Your blog can also include behind-the-scenes stories that help your customers' connection to your brand grow.

7. **Demonstrates expertise.** By regularly creating blog posts that educate and entertain your

readers, you establish your position as an expert in your field.

Marketing is much easier when you're regularly creating content and blogging is often the easiest way to create that content. It gives you something to share on social media, in email newsletters, and to optimize for SEO. But as compelling as all these reasons are to have a blog, there are also strategic reasons why a blog may not be a good fit for your business:

1. **You're not ready to commit to creating content regularly.** If there is one thing that's worse than not having a blog, it's having a blog that's inconsistent or out of date. You don't have to create all of the content yourself, but you do need to commit to creating something.
2. **You only want to focus on your company.** Your blog needs to go beyond promoting your company and provide value for the reader. All the content that you create needs to inspire, motivate, educate or entertain your reader. If you're just looking for another way to get your brand in front of a reader, content creation and blogging aren't going to be the right fit for you.
3. **You're looking for a quick fix.** Blogging isn't a short-term fix for anything in your business.

Just like I mentioned before, blogging is something you need to do consistently. Getting the benefits of better search engine results or "expert" status take time to build up and mature.

Remember, you can always add a blog to your business website later after you've established your MVM strategy and are starting to see results.

Of course, blogging isn't the only way to create unique content for your business. You can also create and share content in other ways, like videos (either on your site or on a YouTube channel) and podcasts. For more resources on creating compelling brand video series and podcasts, check out the additional resources on the website.

**The Technology of Your Website**
Even if you're not into the technical side of building a website and you're going to hire someone to set it up for you, there are a few technical things to be sure that you understand:

**SSL Certificate**
SSL stands for Secure Socket Layer – but don't worry, there's not a quiz on that later. An SSL

certificate is what allows your URL to show up as https:// instead of http://. While that may not seem like a big deal to you, it's a big deal to the search engines, especially if you're collecting any data online, including email addresses or using contact forms.

An SSL certificate is a bit of code on your web server that provides security for online communications. When a web browser contacts your secured website, the SSL certificate enables an encrypted connection. It's kind of like sealing a letter in an envelope before sending it through the mail.

Your web hosting company (like GoDaddy, SiteGround, or WPEngine) should have a tutorial to walk you through adding a certificate to your site if you're setting it up yourself.

## Google Analytics

If you're serious about growing your business online, you need Google Analytics on your website. With Google Analytics, you can learn about who is coming to your site (where they're from, age groups, gender, etc.), how they're getting there (organic search, social media, referral links), and what they're doing while they're there (page flows, bounce rates, etc.).

The best part is Google Analytics is *free* and, in most cases, you can add it to your site in less than 5 minutes. We'll go more in-depth on how to use the information from Google Analytics later in the book.

**Sitemap**

A sitemap is a listing of all of the pages on your website. While a sitemap doesn't seem like it adds much value to you or your users, they're important for search engines. SEMRush has a great listing of tools you can use to generate a Sitemap[vii] and how to submit it to Google and Bing webmaster tools. If your website is built on WordPress and you're using Yoast for SEO, they also have a sitemap generator tool.

**A Mobile Version**

Virtually everyone has a computer in their pocket these days and they're the first tools we pull out when we have a question. Websites that are responsive (which means they adjust well to mobile devices as well as desktops) rank higher in search engine results.

## SEO

SEO is the abbreviation for Search Engine Optimization. SEO is all the things you can do on your website to help it show up when people search for businesses or blogs like yours on Google, Bing, or Yahoo.

SEO includes simple things like your page titles, how often you use keywords, and using alt-tags on your images. It also includes some complicated and technical optimizations and reviews including page load times, engagement metrics, and 302 errors, just to name a few.

We're only going to be covering the basics of SEO here – for a complete guide, I highly recommend the free MOZ Beginner's Guide to SEO.[viii]

## Tips for Beginning SEO

### Spend a little time on research

Build a list of terms that you want your website to rank for. Ideally, these will be long-tail keywords. Long tail keywords are three or four words long that are very, very specific to what you're selling. Long tail keywords they may not get as much traffic as shorter keyword phrases, but a collection of them generates quite a bit. Long-term keywords are easier to rank for. It's going to be hard to bump Wikipedia or Bitcoin out of the top positions for the search term "bitcoin" but with a bit of diligence, you may be able to rank for "how to invest in bitcoin."

**Optimize each page for unique keywords (or key phrases)**
If you've done keyword research, you should have a list of keywords you can use on your website. Each page and post should be optimized for unique keywords or keyphrases. For example, I may want to optimize my entire site for "marketing for solopreneurs." In order to do that, I might try using that phrase on every page, as alt tags on all my images and in all my titles and subheadings.

While this seems like it would guarantee my top ranking for that phrase, it would actually *reduce* the value of my site. There are so many important concepts that go into "marketing for solopreneurs" that there's a treasure trove of additional keywords I could use.

**Avoid keyword stuffing**
When you first start learning about SEO and

keywords, you may be tempted to just put your keyword in as many places as you can. Once upon a time, this worked – the practice was called keyword stuffing. But search engines have gotten smarter. Now you want to create pages and posts for readers, not for search engines. That means using your keyword as often as makes sense, but not to the point where it becomes overwhelming for the readers. According to Yoast (developer of the popular Yoast Wordpress plugin), the ideal keyword density is 0.5-2.5% per page.[ix]

**Use keywords in your title**

Another way to help yourself rank is to use keywords in your titles, including page titles, blog titles, and those subheadings that appear throughout your page. Use them when it's appropriate, without slipping into over-use. Your website content, including headings and subheadings, needs to be written for the reader, not the search engines.

**Use keywords in your image alt-tags**

An alt tag (also known as an alt attribute or alt description) is a text alternative for search engines that is added to an image. Applying alt tags with appropriate keywords to images like product photos can positively impact your site's search engine rankings.

**Link to other relevant content**
Both internal links (links to other pages on your site) and external links (links to other people's websites) are important for your SEO. Internal links help tell search engines which are the most important pages on your website, while external links show that other people's content is important. These external links help you come across as an authority and can help the search engines figure out what your content is about.

For a more in-depth and up-to-date review of SEO, including advanced topics, visit Moz.com or Yoast.com.

# ACTION STEPS

**If You Already Have a Website**

Look through your existing site with the eyes of your customer with the following questions in mind:

- Is the language clear and easy to understand, avoiding industry jargon?
- Does your eye move naturally across the layout?
- Are the images modern, inviting, and relate to your products and services?
- Can you identify the goal of each page? Is it there to serve the customer (or the business owner)?
- Do you know what to do next? Are there clear calls-to-action for next steps (like to schedule a call, make a reservation, or place an order)?

**If You're Just Getting Started with Your Website:**

- Get a pen and paper and sketch out how you expect people to navigate around your site before you start building a single page (or working with a developer or designer to create the pages).

- Clearly identify the goal of each page – what should the reader know or understand after reading the page?
- Decide if you're going to be adding content on a regular basis, through a blog, podcast pages, or video series.

Start figuring out the tech stuff – including picking a content management system (like Wordpress or Squarespace) and hosting for your site. Most "how to build your website" tips start with the tech, but I encourage you to really think about the goals of your website and what you need to accomplish so you can pick the right supporting tools to make it happen.

# Chapter 6
## Email Marketing

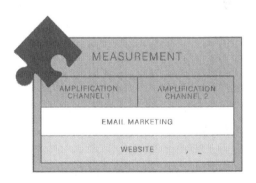

Most business owners fall into one of three camps when it comes to email marketing:

1. I hate getting emails, so I don't send them.
2. I guess I should have an email list, but I don't know where to start.
3. I have a list, but I could be doing more with it.

No matter which of these camps you're in, here's the truth:

1. You need an email list.
2. Your social media following doesn't count.

In this chapter you'll:
[__] Review why email marketing is important for your business
[__] Pick an email service provider
[__] Develop a content strategy for your messaging
[__] Set your email marketing frequency
[__] Build and grow your email contact list
[__] Learn what makes a good email
[__] Understand the difference between an email newsletter and a funnel or automation

## Why Email Marketing is Important for Your Business

Email marketing can be a very simple – or very complex – component of your MVM strategy. You can have one list that you send everything to regularly – simple. Or you can use more sophisticated techniques like segmentation and remarketing – complex.

When you dip your toe in and you start hearing about your lead magnet and funnel, it probably feels much easier to just build a Facebook page, post some offers or news once in a while and call it a day.

That would be the equivalent of building your entire business presence on MySpace. MySpace was at its peak in December 2008 with nearly 76 million users. Even then, Facebook already had more users. MySpace also had 2.57 billion user sessions in per month June 2009. In June 2018, just 9 short years later, that traffic had dwindled to 8.81 million per month.

Sure, 8.81 million sessions is still a lot – more than most of us will have on our business websites. But that's still a decrease of 99.657%. Could your business withstand a decline like that?

And then there are the changes in algorithms on the platforms that are still around. In January 2018, Facebook redesigned their newsfeed to deprioritize business pages that were not generating engagement. It had an immediate impact on publishers and business owners. Some ran off to build Facebook Groups while others decided it was time to learn how to run ads.

What about if you started building your email list in 2008? Sure, there would be a churn of new people coming on and old people dropping off, but it could, and would, still be going strong as long as you nurtured it.

When you focus on building an email list, you're building a portable, permission-based customer list that you can take virtually anywhere.

Email marketing, done correctly, is permission-based marketing at its finest. Your readers have entrusted you with their email address and the permission to use it. They probably gave it to you in a trade agreement where you gave them an extra-special piece of content for that right.

Even if your email service provider (who hosts your list and sends your emails – MailChimp, ActiveCampaign, ConvertKit, Aweber, Constant Contact, etc.) goes out of business, you can still email your list. Instead of the service provider owning the relationship (like Facebook or Instagram does), you own the list.

At any time, you can download your list from one service provider and move over to another. As a matter of fact, many people start with a low-cost provider (like MailChimp) and move to a more advanced system (like ConvertKit or ActiveCampaign) as their list grows and their needs change.

There's an additional level of trust that comes with joining your email list. And with trust, comes dollars. Research shows that someone on your email list is more likely to buy from you than a general social media follower. This stems from the foundation of trust that was started with the opt-in and is enhanced by ongoing engagement.

Let's look at a few stats.

A consultant or trainer can expect a 13.93% open rate and a 7.19% click-through rate on their emails.[x] Compare that to the average engagement rate on Facebook across all industries of 0.17%.[xi]

If you have 1000 Facebook followers, you're likely

to get 1.7 clicks and that's only if they even see your post, given the changes to the newsfeed.

If you have 1000 email subscribers, you're likely to get 71.9 clicks.

You'd need over 42,000 Facebook followers to generate the same number of clicks as 1000 email subscribers.

And those click-through rates are just based on an average. With testing, segmentation, and funnels, you may see even better results. I've seen client emails get 25-30% click-through rates.

Still not convinced?

According to Business2Community, for every $1 marketers spend on email, the average ROI is $40.[xii] That's a 4000% ROI. I've sent email campaigns that have resulted in 6-figure revenue from a single send.

And you don't need to email several times a day. As a matter of fact, you shouldn't email that often. You can achieve these results emailing as infrequently as a couple of times a month or as frequently as a couple of times a week.

Now, with all the advantages of email marketing comes some responsibility.

Email marketing is regulated nationally and internationally with laws like the US CAN-SPAM Regulations, Canadian Anti-Spam Law (CASL), and EU General Data Protection Regulation (GDPR). I will reference these regulations throughout this section, but for the most up-to-date information on how they may be affecting your email marketing strategy, visit the website (MinimiumViableMarketing.com)

## Components of a Healthy Email Marketing Strategy

Now that you're convinced you need to be using email as part of your MVM foundation, it's time to build your email strategy. Here are the basics you need to get started:

## Pick a Service Provider

Email marketing is done through a platform called an email service provider. Unlike your email inbox (like Gmail or Outlook), an email service provider has specific features to help you build and maintain your email list, send professionally designed messages, and measure the results.

Some of the industry-leading email service providers for small businesses include:

- MailChimp
- ConstantContact
- Aweber
- ConvertKit
- ActiveCampaign

*You can see my current recommended resources at minimumviablemarketing.com/tech-stack*

Starting prices for these range from free to $50/month and then increase based on list size and how often you send out emails.

There are also large enterprise providers used by some of the largest companies in the world like American Express, Home Depot, and Disney. These include:

- Salesforce Marketing Cloud (formerly ExactTarget)
- Bronto by Oracle
- Adobe Campaign

For most companies just getting started with email marketing, one of the small business providers will do everything you need and probably more!

Key features that your email service provider should offer:

1. Customizable forms
2. Plugins that work with your website platform, like Squarespace or WordPress
3. Required double opt-ins
4. Basic automation tools (like being able to send a few emails over a few days automatically when someone signs up for your list)

You'll also want to consider your content strategy (which we'll be talking about more later in this chapter), their support, and your budget. Email service providers are not created equally. Even the free or low-cost ones can have significant variability in the quality of the service they offer.

**Develop Your Email Content Strategy**
The big decisions you're going to make about emailing your email list have to do with your business goals. Here are a few things you may want to do:

- Engage readers over a period of time so they buy when your product is available (commonly used if you have a product you sell infrequently, such a live course)
- Engage your readers to buy products now (used if you have a single product or series of products that can be purchased at any time, including affiliate programs)
- Engage your readers so you can sell sponsorships to your list (used if your primary business strategy is to sell advertising and sponsorships)

Notice the big factor all three of these strategies have in common? *They're focused on connecting with your readers.*

Once you know how you want to use your list, decide what you're going to send them:

- **Blog posts** – either the full content or excerpts that drive them to the content.
- **Exclusive content** – this goes above and beyond sending just what you're writing on the blog. Sometimes it's a preview of what's to come, deeper insights about something in

your industry, or even freebies that you're not offering anywhere else.

- **Personal messages** – A personal message may be a lot like your exclusive content, but it's often written more like a letter to a friend than a "newsletter".
- **Promotions** – With all the talk about giving value to your customers, it's easy to forget the reason you're building an email list is to support your business. And the goal of your business is to make money. That means sales and promotions.

Finally, you'll also need to think about how often you're going to send emails to your subscribers. **Ideally, you'll send a minimum of twice a month, but no more than twice a week.**

You don't have to send the same type of message all the time, but it's good for your readers to get used to when they can expect to hear from you and what you're going to message them about. The most common email frequency is weekly, although the final decision is up to you. Send too often, and you'll see your open rates sink and your unsubscribe rates grow. If you don't send often enough, your customers may forget about you in the hustle and bustle of their inboxes.

There are two exceptions to these frequency recommendations:

1.  Some businesses and individuals have daily emails as part of their business model. This is most common when they're time oriented (like the news aggregation email "The Skimm" or tech news aggregation email "The Hustle") or inspirational/prompt driven (like I Am Mantra's daily mantras or Our Daily Bread's daily Christian devotional emails). If you want to send daily emails, make sure you're communicating that up-front to your readers when they subscribe AND that you're truly committed to creating that much content!

2.  Launch and holiday sales periods. When you're launching a new product or have an "open enrollment" period for a program then you're likely to send more frequent emails *just for that limited period of time*. This is also true for the holiday season if you offer giftable products. If you're increasing frequency like this, be sure to let your readers know when the launch is closing, and, if possible, give them a way to opt-out of receiving any further

promotions for that period of time while staying on your email list.

## Growing Your Email List

Now that you know what service provider you're going to use, what you're going to send, and how often, it's time to start growing that list!

Let's start with a quick "what not to do" – import everyone from your existing address book, including your grandma, your college roommate and that guy you sold some trees to on CraigsList that one time.

Another big "what not to do" is *buying* an email list. Once you've set up your website and have a contact form, you may start to get messages from people saying they can get you a list of thousands of users for your campaigns.

In order to comply with legal regulations (CAN-SPAM, CASL, and GDPR to name a few), you need to have an established business relationship or an explicit opt-in before you can add someone to your email list.

An established business relationship is someone who has purchased from you in the past, or that you've had conversations with recently about making a purchase. The best way to add previous business contacts to your list is to send them a personal email (from your business account) that you're starting a new email newsletter and you'd love to have them subscribe. Include the link to your subscription page and some information about what to expect. If they complete the form to subscribe, you'll have their explicit opt-in.

An explicit opt-in is someone has said: "Yes, I want to get emails from you." This happens on your website through a form that either pops-up or is somewhere on your home page. You can also collect sign-ups offline if you have a physical location.

When you're collecting information for your list, collect just the information you REALLY need in order to send them the right kinds of email messages. Fewer fields to fill out (online or offline) increases your conversion rates, plus it minimizes your risk when it comes to data security and compliance with regulations like CAN-SPAM and GDPR.

For any list, I suggest you collect *at least* first name

along with email address. It makes it so much easier to use personalization when you know someone's name. Personalization is a huge factor in increasing your response rates.

Here are a few other things you may want to collect:

- Business name (if you're in a B2B market)
- Favorite location (if you have several physical store locations)
- Birthday (if you're planning on sending birthday promotions like a free dessert!)

Remember, you can always collect more information later through surveys. The idea is to get the minimum amount of information to get started.

**Creating a Lead Magnet to Grow Your Email List**
Lead magnets, also called freebies or opt-ins, have been common in the B2B space for years and are growing in popularity in B2C markets as well. A lead magnet is an extra bonus a subscriber gets when they sign up for your newsletter list. A decade ago, just getting your newsletter was probably incentive enough. Our inboxes were less cluttered and our smartphones (ok, ok, Blackberries) weren't full of social media

notifications and updates. Now you need that extra incentive to get a visitor to give up their elusive email address.

If you sell products or have a retail location, you can offer coupons for an upcoming purchase or even a way to get a free sample. As an online business provider, the list of options is even longer, including:

- eBooks
- Whitepapers
- Checklists
- Worksheets
- Challenges
- Mini-Courses
- Guides
- Online Events, like webinars or seminars
- Free consultations
- Private Groups, like a Facebook Group or Slack Community
- Resource Libraries
- Templates
- Quizzes
- … and almost anything else you can think of!

With all those choices, it can be hard to decide what's going to get the most people to join your list. Here are two key questions to ask before you decide on your incentive:

- What problem or dilemma is the reader currently facing that I can solve?
- What can I create to solve that?

The answers to these questions for a brick & mortar or traditional eCommerce business are probably different than for an online service provider. You can also test different opt-ins to see what gets more people onto your list.

The incentive you create is the foundation for the transactional relationship you'll have with your email subscribers. You want to *wow* them – make them glad they gave you their email address.

**Setting Up Your Lead Magnet**
First, you'll want to describe your lead magnet on your web forms, as well as any other messages that the subscriber can expect to get. For example, an eCommerce shop may have "Get free shipping on your first order and be the first to know about new products and sales!"

If you're testing different lead magnets or have

different magnets for different categories on your website, you'll need to customize each form to describe what the visitor is going to get when they sign up.

After someone signs up for your lead magnet, you need to set up a double opt-in. With a double opt-in, the new subscriber has to click a confirmation link in an email before they're officially added to your list. It helps with deliverability, keeps your list clean(er), and reduces junk addresses on your list (that you end up paying for over time). Most, if not all, email service providers should provide this option when you're setting up your form and welcome series in their system.

The way I like to think of it is this: All that work you put into your lead magnet – you're asking the subscriber for one extra click. Your lead magnet is WORTH that click. If the subscriber isn't willing to give you that click, are they going to be willing to pay for something else later?

You may have some subscribers that expect to get their lead magnet in that first email – the one where you're asking people to confirm their email address. Make sure you customize it to let them know they'll get the lead magnet after they click to confirm their subscription.

Then, deliver that lead magnet in the final confirmation email (not on the thank you page)! This not only gets them confirmed on your list, it gets you a click right away from the first email you sent them. It lets their inbox know "hey, these emails are the good stuff!"

If you have a multi-part lead magnet, like an email course, you'll need to use automations to deliver the content over a series of time. An automation simply sends emails over a specific period of time automatically, so you don't have to remember to send each one manually.

Be sure to download the checklist for setting up your new opt-in from the online resource library at MinimumViableMarketing.com

**Promoting Your Lead Magnet**
Now that you've developed your lead magnet, you'll want to get people to find it. Here are 7 ways to get people to your lead magnet and onto your list:

1. **Add it as an upgrade to your blog posts.** You're already sharing your blog posts on social media and optimizing them for SEO. They can do double-duty for you by growing your list with an embedded lead magnet form. This works particularly well if your lead magnet relates to the subject you're writing about.

2. **Put it in the sidebar of your website.** Most of us have a sidebar on our website with links to our social media profiles, blog categories, and maybe an "about" shortcut. By adding a link to your lead magnet, you'll gain visibility across your site.

3. **Add a link in your navigation.** Beyond just your sidebar, your navigation menu is visible across your whole website. Add a link to your lead magnet landing page to your site navigation to increase visibility.

4. **Share on social media.** Regularly share your lead magnet on your own social media channels. Add a tab to your Facebook page, offer it in Facebook groups (your own and others, as appropriate), link to it in your Instagram profile, etc.

5. **Add it to your social graphics.** Besides just sharing on your social media channels, you can

share info about your lead magnet on your social images, like your Facebook header image and group cover, Twitter header, etc. Then create a pinned post that has the link. It's easy for new subscribers to find you!

6. **Pin it.** If you're pinning your blog posts, you can also pin your lead magnet landing page on Pinterest.

7. **Guest Appearances.** Just like a celebrity who makes the talk show rounds to promote their new movie, you can promote your new lead magnet through guest appearances including guest blogging, podcasting, and Facebook lives.

**Handling Email Addresses You Collect Offline**

If you run a retail store location or exhibit at trade shows or markets, you're likely to collect email addresses in person. You'll need to add these to your email list manually. Create a spreadsheet of all of the email addresses as soon as you can after you've collected them and upload them to your email service provider. For events, like a tradeshow or market, do this as soon as you get back. It should be second in priority only to following up on active sales opportunities. For a physical list you collect in your store, add new subscribers twice a week.

When you upload a list, the email service provider will not send a double opt-in. You should also be able to choose if it sends them a welcome message – which you should.

To stay compliant with email marketing regulations, including CAN-SPAM, GDPR, and CASL, keep the paper records of all email addresses you collected, where they were collected, and when (if you don't like keeping paper around, you can also scan them and file them electronically). If someone did report you as fraudulently emailing them, this paper trail helps you cover your tail.

## Creating Great Emails

Earlier in this chapter, I shared the types of results businesses can get with email marketing. The 42x ROI isn't guaranteed, though. The emails you send to your customers need to be well planned, on-brand, and virtually error-free in order to get the best results.

## Start with a Plan

The first step in creating a good email is having a good plan before you open the email composer.

Pick a single offer or call to action and use it throughout your copy and images. You may be tempted to throw everything you've got into every email, but this actually can do more harm than good. Research has shown that if someone has too many choices, they're actually less likely to buy.

When you're building your email, make sure you consider the following:

- **Subject line:** The subject line makes your email stand out in the inbox. Your tone and voice should be true to your brand, and make someone want to open your message. After all, they can't read and buy from an email that goes straight to the trash folder.
- **Preheader text:** If you're sending HTML emails (the ones that have a lot of formatting and images), then you'll also want to include pre-header text. This is what shows up in the preview in the inbox. It should tease the contents of the email even more to encourage the open.
- **Call to action:** What do you want the subscriber to do after they read your emails? Is it to purchase something? Click through to read an article? Book a call? Pick the desired action BEFORE you start crafting the

message – stick to that primary objective. Having a single call to action helps improve your response rates.

## Don't Say Too Much

The ideal length for an email is 50-125 words, according to a study by Boomerang.[xiii] That doesn't mean you'll get terrible results if your email is 49 words or 127 – but this length is the ideal for driving responses. Over half of emails are opened on a mobile device[xiv], so the shorter messages are easier to read and act on than longer ones. Just don't err on the side of too short – your messages need to communicate enough value to spark interest in taking action.

Word count isn't just for the body of your message either. The ideal length for your subject line is 8 words.[xv]

## Stay on Brand

The tone and design of your emails should align with the core of your brand. While other platforms can have a bit more variability, like the off-the-cuff, behind the scenes videos on SnapChat versus the suit-and-tie tone on LinkedIn, your email content should firmly align with your core messaging. Your email content should strengthen your relationship with your customers and can often provide a valuable two-way communication channel.

## Test Test Test

Avoid that dreaded "Oops! Something went wrong!" email and catch any errors ahead of time. Send yourself a test of each email before you schedule it to send out. Check your copy, links, images, sender information and lists. Be sure to look at how your email displays on mobile as well as on laptop or desktop computers. Don't take the testing for granted - I've emailed over 100,000 people with a misspelled subject line. Mistakes like this are avoidable!

## Email Newsletters vs Funnels/Automations

A lot of people are talking about funnels and automations when it comes to email marketing. These tools are powerful ways to quickly warm people up and get them to buy from you.

So, what's the difference between an email newsletter and a funnel – and how do you know which you need to send?

## What is an Email Newsletter?

An email newsletter is a piece of content you send out on a regular basis – often weekly – but can be as frequent as daily or as infrequent as monthly (I suggest you start on a weekly or bi-weekly basis and then adjust frequency based on what you can create and your readers want to read).

Email newsletters come in many different styles:

- Personal messages
- Blog posts – either full content or a summary/overview and a link to the full message
- Link Round-Ups – either curated content, your own, or a mix
- Promotions – common if you're running a store and aren't doing any of your own content

With an email newsletter, new subscribers can jump in at any time. When you're writing a newsletter, you'll need to remember that not everyone has been with you from the beginning of your journey and frame your content appropriately for both new readers and the readers who have been with you for weeks or months.

**What is a Funnel or Automated Email Series?**
An email funnel is a series of emails that go out on a set schedule, based on when someone took a specific action, like signing up for your opt-in or joining a challenge that you're running. They can last just a few emails, or for quite a while. I've built automations that were over 20 emails long that lasted 3 months.

Unlike an email newsletter, with a funnel, everyone starts at the same point. No matter when someone signs up, they'll receive email 1 right away and move through the series at their own pace. If Sally signs up for your opt-in today, she'll get email 1 in your funnel or automation today, and email 2 in three days. If John signs up for your opt-in in five days, he'll get email 1 that day, and email 2 three days after that. Because of this staggered timing, you'll need to think through any dates that you put into your funnel to make sure they're still relevant.

For example, if you are promoting an upcoming course launch in a funnel series, you'll need to update your funnel after the course has opened to start promoting the next course launch date, the evergreen version, or the wait-list.

**Do You Need an Email Newsletter or a Funnel?**
In most cases, you'll want both an email newsletter and a funnel. A funnel has a specific goal in mind, often driving to a purchase, while the newsletter keeps prospects warm for future campaigns and purchases.

Questions to ask yourself when designing your funnel and email strategy:

1. *Should people who are still in my funnel get my email newsletter too?* Depending on the goal of your funnel and how long it lasts, you may or may not want people to get your email newsletter while they're still part of your funnel. With most email service providers, you can create an action at the end of your funnel to add the subscriber to your newsletter list.
2. *How long should my funnel be?* The longer your sales cycle, the longer your funnel will typically be. For most new welcomes and funnels, I recommend 3-5 messages.
3. *Can I just do a funnel and no newsletter?* The best email strategies have a mix of funnels and newsletters. Remember, funnels are driving to

a specific goal over a limited series of emails, while newsletters nurture and build relationships over the long term.

## Special Email Circumstances

If you're running a membership site or sell online, you may also have emails that fall into the category of transactional emails. These include:

- Forgot my password
- Order Confirmation
- Shipment Confirmation

In many cases, your eCommerce platform (like Shopify or Magento) can be configured to send these messages for you. They'll come with basic templates that use your logo and an email address you provide.

Take the time to customize and update these messages to connect with and delight your customers. While there's specific information that you'll want to keep front and center, like the link to reset the password or an order number, you can rewrite much of the content to align with your brand.

Some of these messages – like shipment confirmations – are great opportunities to ask for a referral or provide a special offer for a follow-up purchase.

By the way, transactional emails are exempt from regulations like GDPR and CAN-SPAM, as they relate to a specific inquiry or transaction.

# ACTION STEPS

Whether you're just getting started with email marketing, or you've been building your list for a decade, your welcome emails are some of the most important emails you'll send. You should send 3-5 emails as part of a welcome series before you start sending standard promotions.

Review (or build) your welcome series using the following framework:

**Welcome Series Message 1**
The first email in your welcome series is the first one they get after they've confirmed their subscription using a double opt-in. In this email, you want to introduce people to your brand, who you are, and you are uniquely qualified to help them.

Your brand story is an opportunity let your new subscriber know that you've been where they are, that you're now on the other side, and that you can help them get there too.

You also want to set expectations of how often they'll be hearing from you and what kind of information you share in your emails.

This email is also a prime opportunity to build a connection with your readers. Ask them a question that drives a response. For example, you can ask them about the biggest problem they're facing now (that relates to your business, of course).

**Welcome Series Message 2**
24-48 hours later, you'll send the second message. In this message, add value and appeal to ways you can fix the problem they had when they signed up. In email 2, give them more ways to connect with you, like following you on social media, joining your Facebook group, or subscribing to your podcast.

This is still the honeymoon phase with your email subscriber, so you'll want to deepen the connection as much as possible. This is also a good time to give a subtle nudge to your product or service.

**Welcome Series Message 3**
The final email in your welcome series will go out 24-48 hours after email two. With this email, we

want to get more information about your subscribers. Ask a question and give a couple of links for someone to answer – then when they click on the link, your email service provider can tag (or label) the subscriber with their preference. You can use this to segment your subscribers to send them special offers – plus you'll learn a lot about who your subscribers are and what they need.

This is also a good time to help people go a bit deeper with you and your content, so include links to 3-5 of your favorite pieces, whether they're from your podcast, video series, or your blog.

This third email is also the prime time to share a short-term or limited time offer. You've built a solid introduction, helped your new subscriber tackle at least a small piece of the problem that they're facing, and given them some good free content. Now give them a way to tackle the issue they're facing with a few dollars.

By doing a small offer now, you also start to train your subscribers from the beginning that you're going to be selling to them. I've seen many clients who have needed to do a lot of clean up on their lists because they were afraid to sell in the beginning. Instead, they kept giving away value, hoping that eventually those people would seek them out and want to pay. Unfortunately, the opposite happened – they kept clamoring for more free help and support.

Your subscribers need to know that this is a business for you and you're going to give them the opportunity to pay you. Some will take you up on it. Some never will. But the more often you give value, the easier it's going to be to get more of them to pay you.

## PART 3
Using Amplification Channels to Expand
Your Reach

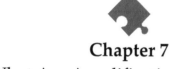

# Chapter 7
# What Are Amplification Channels?

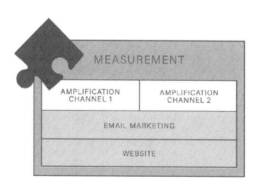

So far, we've focused on the foundation of your MVM strategy. Before you move on to amplifying your reach with the techniques in this section, make sure you've built your foundation. You need somewhere to send the people you connect with on these other platforms.

In this chapter, you will:
[__] Identify the three primary types of amplification channels.
[__] Find the right amplification channels for your strategy.
[__] Learn how to create messaging for your amplification channels.

It's not a case of "if you build it, they will come." We need to leverage appropriate amplification channels to spread your message and increase your visibility.

Most amplification channels fit into one of three categories:

- Social Media
- Search Platforms
- Advertising

Your MVM strategy leverages two amplification channels from any category. You can choose two social media platforms, social media and advertising, or any combination. *This does not mean that you are "stuck" with these platforms forever, or that you can never expand.*

For the next 90 days, these platforms are where you are going to focus your efforts to make the most of your limited time. Don't worry – you'll be seeing results long before those 90 days are up. This focused window gives you the opportunity to maximize your exposure on these platforms and get the best results.

There are many marketing consultants and agencies who advocate being on as many platforms and leveraging as many channels as you can. But with the MVM approach, we'll focus on the amplification channels that:

1. Reach most of your ideal customers
2. Leverage your skill-set and interests
3. Fit within your budget

For example, your ideal clients may spend hours every week scrolling Instagram, but if you don't have an eye for photography or designing share-worthy quote images (and you don't want to pay someone else to do it for you), then Instagram may not be one of your top two platforms.

On the other hand, Twitter could be right up your alley if you love sharing short quips, quotes, and insights several times a day and engaging in fast-moving conversations.

Remember, increasing your reach and amplification is going to take one of two things: time or money. When you're selecting your MVM amplification channels, you'll need to consider this balance.

**Selecting Amplification Channels**

When you're selecting your amplification channels, don't just rely on gut instinct. You'll need to do research and strategic thinking to select the two amplifications that you'll focus on for the next 90 days.

There's a worksheet to help you evaluate amplifications as part of the Resource Library over at MinimumViableMarketing.com. You can print it out or download it and complete it online. Go through the questions each time you're considering adding an amplification channel.

**Research Questions**
- How many active users does it have?
- How many of those active users are within

your target market?
- What format are most posts in - video, graphics, written, etc.?

## Target Market Questions
- How is your audience using this channel? (For example, if their hot water heater goes out in the middle of the night, they're probably not hopping on Facebook to look for a plumber!)
- Does it benefit you (or your customers) for them to interact with each other? (i.e., are they members of a community)

## Preference Fit Questions
- What type of content do you enjoy creating?
- How often can you share content or launch campaigns?
- What is your budget?

## Competitor Questions
- Do your key competitors use this channel?
- How is their reach? Followers? Engagement? Frequency?

You can use any mix of amplification channels to reach your customers. Here are some mixes that I've seen used successfully:

- Facebook Page and Facebook paid advertising
- LinkedIn and PPC Ads
- Facebook and Instagram
- PPC Ads and Twitter
- Instagram & Pinterest

## Messaging for Amplification Channels

When you're selecting amplification channels, consider what you're going to share on those platforms, whether or not you've decided to blog, podcast, or create a video series.

## The Hub & Spoke Model

If you are creating content on a regular basis, you've already got some themes to work with on your amplification channels. I like to think of it as a hub-and-spoke model. Your new content is the hub, and sharing it on amplification channels are the spokes. With a good piece of content, you can create several different spokes for a single amplification platform.

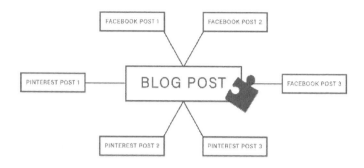

## Curating Content

Whether you're creating your own content or not, curating content is key to filling up your amplification channels. Curating content is the process of finding great content and presenting it to your customers and prospects in a way that's organized, meaningful, and adds value (for the audience and your brand).

That doesn't mean you need to share content from your competitors. Instead, you can curate content from industry leaders and complementary brands. For example, a bookkeeper could share content from the IRS, small business development centers, and even accounting software companies. A massage therapist could share content about meditation, nutrition, or foam rolling and stretching.

Beyond posting a link to the curated content, you should also take this opportunity to demonstrate your own expertise. You can add your own commentary, highlight what you think the article got right, or even disagree with the author (as long as you share why you disagree!).

If you're not creating any original content, like a blog or podcast, you will need to create content for your amplification channels. That may mean taking pictures of your products, writing posts or tips that relate to your product or service, or creating special offers to go with your advertising campaigns.

# Chapter 8
## Social Media Channels

For most business owners, the first type of amplification channel that comes to mind is social media. After all, social media has transformed how we spend our time, how we connect with others, and often how we make decisions.

Social media is also big business. In 2018, social media ad revenues were forecast to exceed $22B (Statista.com). That doesn't take into consideration the full revenue impact of the social media ecosystem, like independent social media managers, the increased spend on graphic design and videography, agencies dedicated to developing social media presence, and information products related to making the most of social media.

The biggest platforms for businesses in 2018 include Facebook, Instagram, Twitter, and LinkedIn (for the purposes of this section, Pinterest and YouTube are search channels).

Rather than do a deep dive into these platforms which would likely be out of date by the time this book is published, you can head over to MinimumViableMarketing.com for more up-to-date information on each platform.

Overall, all social media platforms provide opportunities for organic engagement and growth as well as paid advertising options. As I mentioned before, success takes an investment of either time or money (or both). While you can certainly build your social presence purely through organic (unpaid) efforts, you may also want to add periodic small tests of paid advertising to speed your results.

Do not replace organic efforts with paid ads, however. While paid techniques drive engagement or conversions for a specific promotion, ongoing organic activity, including regular posts, will help you build and sustain relationships with followers over time. Once you have established a strong organic reach, you'll discover better results at a lower cost using paid ads.

When you're evaluating social media platforms as part of your amplification strategy, you'll likely find that your ideal customers are using those platforms. After all, Facebook has over 2 billion active users each month across virtually every age group and demographic.

Unfortunately, that doesn't mean it's the right place to connect with them. Let's say you run into your doctor at the golf pro shop (or craft store – whatever floats your boat). Would you want them to come up and ask how that rash is doing? *Probably not!* That's what it's like when you try to connect with your clients in a place they're not ready to find you.

Here are a few questions to ask yourself before embarking on a social media journey:

- Are my customers likely to want to connect

with each other? (If your product or service is for a sensitive issue, the answer to this may be no)

- Do I help people reach their goals for using the platform (i.e., foster sense of community or belonging, organizing events, connecting with friends and family?)
- Do I have time to maintain social media profiles, including creating new posts and responding to comments? *Remember, it's better to have no presence than a lackluster one.*

If you answered yes to all three of these questions, social media may be a good choice for you. In this case, you'll need to pick your platforms and develop your strategy.

## Goal Setting for Social Media

Whether you're investing cold, hard cash into paid social media strategies, seemingly infinite time for organic engagement, or a combination of the two, you need to have clear, impactful goals and metrics to track those goals for each channel. For example, if your goal is to increase brand awareness, you may track follower counts, post engagement trends, link clicks, or website referral analytics.

It's easy with social media to focus on numbers

that make us feel like we're accomplishing bigger things than we actually are. Your follower count doesn't matter if those followers aren't engaging with your brand to truly amplify your message.

| VANITY METRICS | VALUE METRICS |
|---|---|
| FOLLOWERS<br>LIKES<br>SHARES<br>VISITORS<br>PAGE VIEWS | ROI<br>CONVERSION RATE<br>CUSTOMER LIFETIME VALUE |

This is why it's important to identify how you're going to measure your goals. If your goal is simply brand awareness, then the metrics of followers, likes, and shares are valuable. If you're working to drive registrations for an upcoming event or purchases of a new product, your metrics need to focus more heavily on conversion rate.

The MVM method is focusing on building the opportunity for long-term customer relationships. This means one goal of every campaign needs to be a conversion to your email list.

As discussed earlier in this chapter, any social

media amplification platform can change their model (or close completely) in the blink of an eye – taking all of those followers, likes, and shares with them. By carefully tracking the email subscription conversion goal, you can ensure that your work sticks around – even if the platform doesn't.

If you're running paid campaigns – no matter what your budget – you'll want to check in more frequently than the recommended weekly tracking. Be sure to get your social campaign tracking spreadsheet at MinimumViableMarketing.com.

## Social Media Strategies

While each social media platform will have its own nuances in terms of driving engagement, the same basic strategies apply to all social platforms:

1. **Be consistent with your brand.** While your entire feed doesn't need to be a cookie-cutter version of your previous posts, it's good to create some consistency with the colors, fonts, and styles that you want to leverage. For example, on Instagram, you can pick 2-3 filters for photos and use them consistently rather than doing a different filter for every post.

2. **Post consistently, if not frequently.** Social media is one of the fastest-moving amplification platforms, so in order to reach your ideal customers, you'll need to be showing up regularly. The home page (web or app) on all the platforms is a hybrid of most-recent and most-popular posts. Create posts that encourage sharing and commenting to keep your brand top-of-mind with customers.

3. **Engage with your network**. These platforms are called *social* networks for a reason. They're not just places to broadcast your messages. Follow your followers to learn more about their needs and interests, respond quickly to direct messages and questions, and ask questions or leverage polls to get more feedback. Be sure to engage with others in complementary markets as well to expand your brand presence. In fact, many platforms including Facebook are prioritizing posts that provide "meaningful engagement."[xvi]

4. **Curate content**. Go beyond sharing your own content by selecting the best content from thought leaders in your industry. Not only does curated content make it easier to fill up your feed, but it also provides a valuable

service to your followers by sharing only the best of the best.

5. **Connect with influencers**. Influencers are individuals who have authority in your target market. You can share original content from influencers, respond to their questions, and leverage appropriate hashtags to get their attention. Once you have their attention, continue to engage with them and their content to encourage them to become brand ambassadors.

Social media isn't right for every business or every business owner. There are many other methods for amplifying your message and reaching your target customers if you choose not to use social media personally or professionally.

# Chapter 9
## Search Platforms

SEO (search engine optimization) affects how find-able your business is on traditional search engines like Google and Bing search. You can also choose to add your content to other sites where people leverage search to find new content.

Two of the biggest content hubs are YouTube and Pinterest. Different than content aggregators which simply collect content from other websites (often using RSS feeds), Pinterest and YouTube allow you to create profiles and select content to share.

Local search sites like Yelp, TripAdvisor and, Google My Business also offer profiles that local business owners can claim and optimize to improve their ranking in traditional and on-site search results.

## YouTube

YouTube is the video aggregation powerhouse. Whether you're looking for cute baby sloth videos, crochet tutorials, or the latest Marvel movie trailer, there's a video (*or 500*) for you on YouTube.

So why would you want to put your business on YouTube? Well, it's the second most visited website in the world.[xvii] And according to Think with Google, 68% of YouTube users watched YouTube to help make a purchasing decision.[xviii]

You don't need a lot of expensive equipment to create good video content. You can record video with your smartphone or your computer's built-in video camera and a good microphone. If you don't want to be on camera, you can create slides that you show on-screen with your narration. If you're showing how to do something on the computer, you can also record what's happening on-screen with programs like Zoom or Loom.

If you're creating videos as your primary content profile, consider creating your own YouTube channel. Almost 2 billion people in 90 countries watch videos on YouTube every month. YouTube already reaches more 18-49-year-olds than any cable network and it won't cost you cable network prices to reach them.

**Keys to success on YouTube**

The name of this section is search platforms – and that's what YouTube is. Just like you need to consider a few technical things like keywords and meta-descriptions when optimizing your website, you'll also need to leverage titles, descriptions, keywords, and tags to help users find your content.

1. **Use short, snappy titles that use your keywords.** Whenever you're writing a title and cover art, ask yourself, "Would I click on this if I didn't know the brand?" Keep revising your title until the answer is yes.
2. **Ask for the subscription.** While you'll get a lot of views from search, especially for evergreen or pillar videos, subscribers are important on YouTube. At the close of videos, remind

people how they can subscribe to your channel and get access to more, similar content.

3. **Stay on brand.** Everything on your YouTube channel – from your video cover images to your content – should align with your brand. If your brand is lighthearted, make sure that comes through in your videos. On the other hand, if your brand is buttoned-up, make sure your videos reflect that as well.

4. **Work from a consistent publishing schedule.** Even on search-based platforms, you'll want to be publishing new work consistently. Whether it's a single highly-produced video once per month or daily vlogs, train your subscribers (and yourself) to know when they can expect new content.

5. **Engage with your fans.** In the course of your videos, encourage readers to share their thoughts in the comments – and then actually make the time to read and respond. When people feel like they have access to the person behind a brand, their loyalty skyrockets.

6. **Share your channel on other platforms.** The YouTube algorithms work similarly to social media, with the most viewed videos moving up the ranks of search engine results. You can embed videos as blog posts on your website (with optimization, of course), share them with

your email subscribers, and on other amplification channels as appropriate.

If you're creating a lot of content for your brand, you may be thinking of YouTube as just the hosting platform so you can embed videos on your website or share links on other amplification platforms. But even if you're simply using YouTube as your video hosting service, still invest time optimizing your profile, creating good video covers and good descriptions. Even if YouTube is not a primary amplification channel for you, you can still gain a wider audience (and improve brand credibility) with just a small amount of extra effort.

**Pinterest**
Pinterest describes themselves as an online pinboard where people can discover new ideas and find inspiration to do the things they love. As a business leader, it's a visual search engine that allows you to share your best content in visual format.

With over 50 billion pins on over a billion boards, shared and saved by over 200 million users, Pinterest has blazed past many other platforms to drive 5% of total web referral traffic.

Pinterest has also become a platform for eCommerce and shopping – up to 93% of pinners use Pinterest to plan purchases.

Beyond just providing traffic for your website, you can also use Pinterest to keep track of new and upcoming trends in your market, drive email subscriptions (by pinning your lead magnets), and keep tabs on your competition.

NOTE: Even if you're not using Pinterest as one of your amplification channels, you should use Rich Pins and create Pinnable images for your content. This allows your visitors to amplify for you – even if you're not active on the platform!

One successful client of mine discovered she was getting 40% of her site traffic from Pinterest – and she had never pinned before! Readers who were finding her content from social media and SEO were sharing it on Pinterest organically, generating her new traffic and new leads.

**Keys to Pinterest Success**
1. **Use Rich Pins.** Rich Pins provide more information to the user than a traditional pin.

Several different styles of Rich Pins are available, including recipe Pins and article Pins. You can learn more about Rich Pins from Pinterest at https://business.pinterest.com/en/rich-pins

2. **Create great Pin descriptions.** Don't just repeat the title of your article – make use of your Pin description to encourage action. You can improve search results with keyword rich descriptions and hashtags.

3. **Use an on-brand Pin template.** While each Pin should vary slightly, having a standard template that leverages your brand colors and includes your logo will help you streamline Pin creation and help followers recognize your Pins in their feed.

4. **Repin content.** One of the superpowers of Pinterest is that virtually everything you add has the potential to become evergreen content. You can increase the visibility of your Pins by repining them often to both your own boards and group boards.

5. **Join related group boards.** Group boards allow you to get your Pins in front of even more viewers. Be sure to follow the rules of the group board to maintain your membership. Good group boards should also give you

plenty of content to pin for your followers. You can find group boards through influencers in your niche or your analytics, or create your own.

6. **Use a scheduling tool.** Consistency is important in keeping your Pins in front of potential customers. To generate traffic, you'll want to pin up to 20 times per day – with a mix of your own Pins and complementary Pins on appropriate boards. With a scheduling tool like Tailwind, you can preplan a week or further in advance to keep your followers engaged and cycle your own Pins as well.

### Niche & Local Search Platforms

Beyond YouTube and Pinterest, there are also niche and local search channels on which you can share your content. These include Houzz for home décor, Trippy for travel, and Craft Gawker for craft ideas. If your business has a local focus, you may also be able to contribute content as well.

Local search platforms include Yelp, TripAdvisor, and Google Local. While these sites are less about adding your content to the platform, they provide a powerful presence for local businesses. If you have a physical location, be sure to claim your listing and optimize it with professional photos of your space and products, up-to-date contact information, and appropriate details like menus or service listings. Encourage customers and visitors to leave you five-star reviews with signs in your store or on your receipts.

# Chapter 10
## Advertising

The third type of amplification channel is advertising. While advertising can be an add-on strategy for other amplification channels, it can stand-alone with several different valuable types of advertising to consider.

**Why paid advertising?**
Paid advertising is a powerful tool when you're working to reach a niche audience in a short amount of time. As I've mentioned before – all success will take either time or money. When you're short on time, you'll need to ramp up your financial investment.

With today's digital self-service advertising channels, you can gain powerful insights into performance and easily manage your budget to avoid overspends. Unlike mass media advertising like television or radio or outdoor ads like billboards, you don't have to plan weeks or months in advance. You can get started in an afternoon for less than the cost of a nice dinner out.

## Types of Digital Self-Service Advertising

### Search Ads
Search ads are probably one of the first ad types that you thought of for this channel. Search ads are run by search engines, like Google and Bing, alongside organic search results.

These paid ads are sold on a cost-per-click (CPC) basis, which means you pay each time someone clicks on your ad (not every time it displays). The placement is based on an auction basis – so the more you're willing to pay for each click, the better your placement will be. The price of keywords can vary dramatically – from over $50 for keywords in the "insurance" industry to just a few cents for long-tail keywords in niche industries.

Search ads are primarily targeted based on keywords that someone is searching for – although you can also add specific demographic parameters as well including location targeting for local businesses.

To be successful with search ads, you'll need to know some of the keywords that people use when they're looking for your business. Some may be easy – like "dog grooming near me", while others could be more complicated. The search ad platforms like Google Adwords have tools to help you identify the keywords that your customers are using, including Google Keyword Planner.

You'll also need to write ads that meet the platform guidelines and appeal to your target clients. Make sure you include a benefit statement and a clear call to action. You can create multiple versions of your ad to see which performs the best.

In most cases, you can get search display campaigns running in just a few hours.

## Display Ad Networks

Graphic ads that appear on content sites – often in sidebars or even intermixed in the content are often displayed as part of a display ad network. The Google Ad network, one of the largest in the world, displays ads on over 2 million websites and claims to reach up to 90% of internet users.

There are also niche display networks that leverage specific platforms or reach specific niche audiences. For example, Airpush.com focuses on mobile advertising, Midroll places ads during podcasts, and HealthyAds reaches health, wellness and fitness verticals.

The easiest way to find niche display networks is through a search. Websites that show ads from display ad networks may have information on their Contact Page or Privacy Policy.

Display ads are often priced based on impressions (cost-per-thousand, or CPM), although some networks also do a CPC basis.

Graphic ads come in several standard sizes and need to be smaller than a specific file size in order to not slow down the website from loading. Most common ad sizes include leaderboards (728x90 -

or their smaller cousins, banners, 468x60), rectangles (300x250 or 336x280), and skyscrapers (120x600 or 160x600). The size of the ads that you'll need to create will depend on your placement and availability within your ad network.

**Social Media Advertising**
As I mentioned under the discussion of social media channels, most platforms also offer a form of paid advertising. Many of these ads are also sold on a cost-per-click or cost-per-thousand/impressions basis and leverage a combination of text and graphics to have the highest impact.

Social media platforms have a wealth of information about their users – not just from the information that we willingly give them (like our relationship status and age) but from what they learn about our behaviors – other companies we follow, what we like, what we hide from our newsfeed. Using this data, you can build ad campaigns that reach highly targeted audiences – often giving better results than broad campaigns.

**Remarketing**
You've probably already seen these - when you've

checked out a great new pair of shoes, and then you're reading the news and those exact shoes show up in the sidebar – that's a remarketing ad.

Remarketing works by placing a cookie on the site visitor's computer, that the ad network on another website can then see, and show them an associated ad.

Remarketing to those customers using retargeting ads helps bring those visitors back to your site so they can complete their conversions. It increases the effectiveness of all your other marketing efforts, increases your brand awareness, and - most importantly - drives conversions.

Statistically, retargeted display ads get 10x better click-through rates than standard display ads (0.7% for retargeted ads compared to 0.07% for standard display ads, according to CMO).

One downside of retargeting is that you'll need to have enough traffic to your website initially to build your remarketing list – up to 1000 people for some networks. You can, however, use remarketing in combination with traditional advertising to increase your reach and increase brand awareness with new site visitors.

Several paid networks offer remarketing programs, including the Google Ad Network, Facebook, Twitter, LinkedIn, and Instagram.

**Private Advertising Opportunities**
Beyond the DIY options, you can also find opportunities to advertise with private business owners, including bloggers and social media influencers. Often these ads are sold in packages with an amount of time that your ad will run or a specific number of social media posts. They won't guarantee a volume of impressions or results.

If you're considering private advertising opportunities, make sure you ask for a copy of the media kit and references from other advertisers. Verify their statistics including page views through a site like SimilarWeb or Ahrefs, and ask the references how easy the person was to work with through the ad campaign.

To be successful with influencers, you need to treat the relationship as a partnership rather than just a transaction. The power of private advertising opportunities and influencer marketing is the relationship the influencers have developed with their audiences; working with them over the long term allows you to leverage that relationship to benefit your brand.

I've done very successful placements with private advertising opportunities – many of which have resulted in content that my client could leverage after the paid partnership was over.

**Picking the Right Advertising Platform**
While the biggest platforms, like Google Ads or Facebook, may be the easiest to get started with, don't overlook the opportunities with niche platforms to reach a more highly targeted audience.

To pick the right platform for your business, consider the following questions:

- **Are people actively looking for your business or the solutions you provide?** If your target customers are searching for your business – like looking for a hair stylist, dog training, or a keto meal plan, then using a search platform is a good choice. On the other hand, if your product is more of a spontaneous purchase, then display ads or private advertising may be a better fit.

- **What is your budget?** Search ads and social media ads that are sold based on how many clicks they get or times they have seen can allow you to get more reach for a smaller budget, while display ads and private advertising are often more expensive. You can also manage your budget more efficiently, turning ads on and off as you need.

- **Does it reach your target audience?** For each advertising platform, find out if you can narrow the focus to reach your ideal customers. This is especially important if you have a limited geographic reach, like local businesses.

## Keys to Success with Advertising

While every platform needs a strong strategy to succeed, advertising is one channel where you can waste a lot of time and money quickly if you're not paying attention. In fact, I've seen clients spend upwards of $40,000 on search campaigns with no ROI because they didn't develop a cohesive strategy from the beginning.

- **Start with the goal in mind.** Whether you're working on building your email list, generating registrations for an upcoming event, or aiming for direct sales in your eCommerce store, your MVM advertising strategy needs to start with a clear, ROI driven goal in mind.

- **Monitor your budget.** While online ad spend can seem pretty small at first – "Only $1.00 a click!" – but those clicks can add up quickly! Set a small daily or weekly budget to start, and add scale once you're starting to see positive results. If you're working with influencers or private advertising, try to test a smaller-scale program before you make a large investment.
- **Select the right keywords and demographics.** Go back to your ideal customer profile and customer journey to select the audience with the most impact. Use research tools from your selected platform and Google Keyword Planner to create a targeted list of keywords or a demographic profile. Use long-tail keywords (3-4-word phrases) and specific demographics to get the maximum impact for the lowest price.
- **Design compelling ads and optimized landing pages.** Your paid ad campaigns are

not the time to skimp on design or copywriting efforts or make careless mistakes. Test several different varieties of ads and landing pages to identify the mix that gets the best results.

- **Test and optimize.** Paid advertising gives you a great deal of information about how your ads are being seen and interacted with. Testing can include trying out different headlines, different calls-to-action, colors, and more. (Be sure to check out Chapter 17 for more information on how to create a good test.) For each iteration of the ad, you'll be able to see how many impressions it received (i.e., how many times it was seen), and how many times it was clicked on. By pairing this information with your conversions, you'll be able to calculate your cost-per-conversion and optimize your campaigns. *Cost per conversion is calculated by taking the total cost of your ad campaign and dividing it by the number of conversions (i.e., email signups or sales) that the campaign generated.)*

# Chapter 11
## Alternative Amplification Channels

This is not the complete list of all amplification channels you can choose from – they're just the most commonly used across most businesses. The following alternative amplification channels can increase your reach, help you build rapport with your target customers, and build your business.

**Communities**
There are hundreds of free and paid communities that attract like-minded members. Whether you're targeting an audience of new entrepreneurs who want to quit their jobs, homeschooling moms, or comic book enthusiasts, there's likely an online

community that brings them together.

One word of caution about these communities – since it is a community, in most cases you'll need to provide value and develop relationships rather than post blatant promotions. In fact, some communities prohibit self-promotion, making them a better channel for market research than getting customers.

## Outbound Prospecting

Outbound prospecting is the process of reaching out to a targeted list of people (either through email, phone, or both) who haven't had any previous contact with your business. This goes beyond cold-calling from a phone list of the 1990s, though. Modern outbound prospecting leverages in-depth research into key target markets to develop your list and analytics-driven messaging cadences. Outbound prospecting typically works best for business-to-business markets.

The thought-leader in modern outbound prospecting is Aaron Ross, author of *Predictable Revenue*. If you're considering outbound prospecting as an amplification channel for your business, *Predictable Revenue* is a must-read.

### Offline Amplification

There is still plenty of business – and marketing – done offline, particularly for local businesses. This can be in the form of "outdoor advertising" like billboards and bus stops, direct mail, festivals, and conferences. If you're evaluating an offline or local opportunity, be sure to find out about visibility, follow-up opportunities, and results that others have seen who are in a similar market. Many paid offline opportunities are better for brand awareness than driving direct sales.

The easiest way to identify offline marketing opportunities in your area is to pay attention to the marketing you see and receive. For example, most bus shelters and billboards have a company name (other than the sponsor's ad) that you can contact. Your mailbox is also full of direct mail pieces, local magazines, and coupon books.

### Referrals & Repeat Customers

No discussion of amplifying your message and building your customer base would be complete without talking about referrals and repeat customers. Leveraging your existing customers shouldn't be an optional amplification channel. Working with your existing customers, asking for referrals, and encouraging follow-up purchases should be part of your business and customer relationship management strategy.

Some common ways to encourage referrals and repeat customers include loyalty programs to encourage repeat customers, and affiliate and referral programs to attract new customers.

- **Loyalty programs:** Loyalty programs are designed to keep people coming back for more. Whether it's a frequent buyer card at your local pizza shop or the points you accumulate from your online video rentals, loyalty programs reward customers for continuing to shop with you.
- **Affiliate and referral programs:** While loyalty programs encourage the same customer to keep shopping with you, affiliate and referral programs encourage existing customers to share about your business with new potential customers. These programs often pay the existing customer when a new customer makes a purchase – either in the form of discounts, free products/services, or cash.

Beyond formal programs, be sure to ask your customers for reviews and testimonials that provide social proof of your service or product and give you strong content for future marketing messages.

For more on referral marketing and finding repeat customers, you'll find additional reading recommendations on the website (MinimumViableMarketing.com).

# ACTION STEPS

1. Pick **two** amplification platforms to focus on for the next 90 days.
2. Remember, you can select any mix of platforms – whether that's two social media platforms, two advertising platforms, a social platform and a search platform. The key is to select the platforms that effectively reach your target clients when and where they are looking for a solution.
3. After you've picked your platforms, plan your messages and where users will go when they click-through (blog post, custom landing page, sales page, etc.)
4. Pause platforms that are not part of your short-term strategy, if necessary. Pause ad campaigns and create posts on social platforms encouraging visitors to connect on your active channels or join your email list.

BRANDI C. JOHNSON

# PART 4
## Tracking And Metrics

# Chapter 12
## Action-Oriented Metrics

*"What gets measured gets managed."* – Peter Drucker

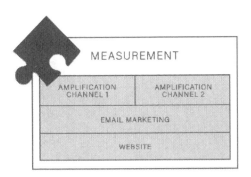

Love this quote or hate it – the truth in marketing

is you *need* measurement to be on track. The days of running your marketing on gut instinct are over.

When you're running an MVM strategy, you'll be measuring your results regularly to make sure you're on track. Don't worry – you don't have to check out numbers every day (unless you want to). Just once a month – and once you've developed a rhythm it should take 30 minutes or less!

You're probably used to measuring financial metrics for your business – income and expenses, and calculating tax payments. Your marketing metrics are just as important as they're often the leading indicators of how those income reports are going to look. Eventually, you may even find that you enjoy looking at your marketing results so you can see how much you're improving!

Before we dive into the metrics that you'll be tracking based on your platforms, be sure to download the metric tracking spreadsheets at minimumviablemarketing.com.

## Tracking Action-Oriented Metrics
There are thousands of metrics you can track in

your marketing – from page views to subscribers to views on every single social media post. You could tumble down the rabbit hole (like I have dozens of times) and start looking at what operating systems are being used by the people visiting your website from half-way around the world.

Luckily for you, I've found my way out of those rabbit holes so you can avoid them. We're going to break down the most important metrics to look at for your foundation and amplification channels so you can get the information you need without developing analysis paralysis with all the data you don't need.

Not all metrics are created equal. It's easy to get caught up in the numbers that make us feel good, like tracking page views and social media followers, ignoring the real indicators of how well our business is doing – like conversions and click-throughs.

That's not to say that these feel-good metrics aren't valuable. After all, someone can't convert on your landing page if they don't visit your landing page. You can't measure a click-through rate without having email subscribers. And you want all of those to be increasing as a sign that your marketing efforts are working.

**Spend Smarter**

Metrics are not just numbers that boost your ego. You'll actually be able to start spending smarter – both your financial investments and your time investment. I've seen clients double their incoming leads by optimizing their ad campaigns and save money in the process. They were also able to spend less time managing their ad campaigns because they were running fewer with better results.

**Maximize Reach**

You'll also find ways to improve your reach. In some cases, you'll find new sources of traffic that you're not leveraging (like my client who discovered she was getting traffic from Pinterest, even though she wasn't pinning her own content.)

In other cases, you'll see that you need to change your strategy. One client I was working with discovered their organic LinkedIn posts were generating 4x the amount of traffic to their website as their Twitter posts, even though they were spending more time and creating more content for

Twitter. By reviewing these metrics, they decided to post more often on LinkedIn and change what they were posting on Twitter to try to get better engagement.

**See Trends**
Tracking your metrics regularly also lets you get ahead of trends. Rather than waiting until the news breaks that a social media or search engine has changed their algorithm, you'll be able to see the impacts on your business ahead of time. And you won't just see trends that are negative. You'll also see when something is improving so you can capitalize on it.

For example, you may see that an older blog post is starting to get more visits from organic search. You can then update that post with more up-to-date information or a fresh call to action to capitalize on your free traffic.

In the following chapters, you'll learn more about the specific metrics you should track for your website, email list, and amplification channels. But there are also a couple of general metrics that you should track of your business as a whole:

- **Cost Per Lead**: This is an important metric to track for your efforts as a whole, not just for each individual channel. To determine your cost per lead, you'll divide your total marketing spend for the period (including advertising costs, marketing tool expenses, and any labor costs) by the number of leads you collected during that same time period. Overall, you want your cost per lead to decrease over time as your marketing gets more effective.
- **Cost per Customer**: Since a lead doesn't always convert into a customer, also track your cost per customer. The calculation is similar to the cost per lead, but instead of using the number of leads during the time period, use the number of new customers.
- **Customer Value**: This metric is more than just a marketing metric; it helps you make key decisions in your business, like how much you can afford to spend on customer acquisition and retention. To calculate this, you'll need to know the average purchase value and the average purchase frequency. Then, multiply these together to get your customer value.

Now, let's dive into specific metrics for each of

your platforms.

# Chapter 13
## Website Metrics

The best tool to collect website metrics is Google Analytics. Google Analytics is a service that lets you track traffic to your website and what people do once they get there and it's free to get started.

To use Google Analytics, you must create an account with Google and install some tracking code on your website.[xix] You only have to do this once in order to track all of your visitors and their behavior.

Google Analytics gives you volumes of data about your website visitors. You can get insights into where your visitors live, what technology they use, including devices, operating systems and browsers, and how they move through your site once they're there.

When you're early in building your business, all this may not seem very important to you. It may not feel great to log in and see that you've gotten 20 page views this week. Over time, you'll see growth from your efforts – and you'll be glad you have those "before" pictures to measure progress and results.

Google Analytics also gives you insights into how people are finding your site (referrals), and what pages are converting best. These are important data points in measuring the effectiveness of your MVM strategy.

**Google Analytics Glossary**
The first time (or even the hundredth time) you look at Google Analytics, you'll notice it seems to speak a language all of its own. Here are some of the most common metrics that Google Analytics tracks and what they mean in real life.

If you're really interested in learning more about

Google Analytics and what all these metrics mean, Google offers free courses through Google Analytics Academy.[xx]

**Session:** A session is a single visit to your website from a single person. That one session includes everything they do during that visit, including visiting multiple pages, buying something, signing up for a newsletter, etc. By default, Google keeps the session open for 30 minutes, so if someone sticks around longer, it would count as 2 sessions.

**Pageview:** A pageview is just like what it sounds like – the view of a page on your website. With Google Analytics, you can see how many times any page on your site was viewed.

**User:** A user is a unique person (or a unique computer) who visits your website. One user can have multiple sessions, and each session can have multiple page views.

**Bounce Rate:** The bounce rate is the percentage of sessions that have a single page view. (A session with a single page view is a bounce.) Bounce rate is one of the things you have to look at knowing your site goals. For example, if you're a lifestyle blog, you may want readers to get hooked and read a lot of articles, and a low bounce rate. On the other hand, if you've got a 1-page informational website with a "call me" call to action, your bounce rate is going to be 100%.

**Session Duration:** If a session is a visit to your website from a single person, the session duration is how long that visit lasts. Session duration is an average of all the sessions that take place during the time frame you're reporting on.

**Traffic Sources:** This is how people are getting to your website. It includes direct (they typed in your URL), organic search (the results in a search based on your optimization), paid search (Google Adwords), social (Facebook, Twitter, etc.), and "Other" (frequently other paid channels).

**Referrals:** This is more detailed information about where your traffic is coming from than just traffic sources. If traffic sources say "Social", referrals will tell you that you got traffic from m.facebook.com, l.facebook.com, and facebook.com.

**Goals:** There's no getting away from goals, even in your analytics. You can create goals in Google

Analytics to track actions you want users to take on your website. They're great for actions like subscribing to your email newsletter, submitting a contact form or registering as a member.

Of course, this isn't a comprehensive list of everything you're going to find in the tangled web of Google Analytics. But most of the rest of them are pretty self-explanatory, as long as you've got these basics covered.

**Setting Goals in Google Analytics**
Google Analytics Goals allow you to track things like:

- eCommerce Conversions
- Lead Conversions
- Email Subscriptions
- Account Creations
- Downloads (like when someone registers for one of your opt-ins/lead magnets)

Sure, you can piece together some data from other sources – you can look at page views in Google Analytics and your new subscribers in ActiveCampaign, but you won't get the whole picture. A goal in Google Analytics for new subscribers will let you dig into cool stuff like what referrals/sources are getting you the most subscribers and even which blog posts. You'll be able to see how many pages people looked at – and what pages – they saw before they completed their purchase.

This is important to MVM because it's not just about what drives the most traffic – it's about what drives you the best RESULTS. Goals = results.

*You only get 20 goals in Google Analytics, so use them wisely!*

The two goals I recommend every business owner set up are email subscriptions and eCommerce conversions (if you're selling directly on your site). These two goals can be used to optimize every page on your site for the goal of increasing your network or increasing your bottom line.

**Tracking Website Analytics**
Each month you'll track the following:

- Users
- Sessions
- Pageviews

- Pages / Session
- Bounce Rate
- Referral Source/Medium 1
- Referral Source/Medium 2
- Goal 1
- Goal 2

Users, sessions, page views, pages/session, and bounce rate can all be found on Audience > Overview. Referral Source/Medium is under Acquisition > All Traffic > Source/Medium. Finally, you can find your goals under Conversions > Goals > Overview.

These statistics make sure that you're getting more traffic to your website (users & sessions), that they're spending more time there (page views, pages/session, bounce rate), and that they're doing what you want them to while they're there (goals). By keeping track of your referral sources, you'll also start seeing the impact of your amplification channels on driving traffic back to your site.

If you've got a bit of extra time and enthusiasm, here are some other metrics I like to check on a monthly basis:

- Audience > Behavior > New vs Returning

Visitors: If your business relies on repeat customers, this stat will help you see if you're retaining your customers or not.

- Acquisition > Social > Conversions: If you're using social media as one of your amplification channels, then you'll want to track your conversions from social platforms.
- Site Content > All Pages: This metric is one of my favorite rabbit holes. You can see statistics on any and every page of your website including how many times it's been viewed, how long people are spending on that page, how often people get to that page – and how often that's the last page they see.

Remember, there's a template tracking for all of these statistics in your MVM Resource Library.

# Chapter 14
## Email Marketing Metrics

The second part of your foundation is email marketing, which comes with its own set of measurements and metrics. Once you start sending messages – even just the confirmation messages for your opt-in – you're going to start getting data about how well your messages are performing. Here are some of the key metrics you need to know (and track):

**List Size:** How many people are on your list. This will change over time – hopefully continuing to grow as you acquire new subscribers. If your list numbers start to decrease, you may need to monitor how many people are unsubscribing from your list.

**Opens/Open Rate:** How many people opened each message (also sometimes called a campaign). The open rate measures how many people – you guessed it – opened your email. The Open Rate is how many unique people opened your email divided by the number of people who email was sent to.

Open Rate = (# of unique opens ÷ # of delivered emails) x 100
(50 unique opens ÷ 150 delivered emails) x 100 = 33% Open Rate
The average open rate across all industries (according to MailChimp) is 20.81%.[xxi]

**Clicks:** How many people clicked on a link in your email.

**Click Thru Rate:** How many people clicked on a link in your email divided by the number of people your email was sent to.

Click Thru Rate = (# of unique clicks ÷ # of delivered emails) x 100

(25 clicks ÷ 150 delivered emails) x 100 = 16.67% CTR

MailChimp reports that the average click rate for all industries is 2.43%.[xxii]

**Click to Open Rate:** How many people clicked on your link divided by the number of people who opened your email. I prefer this metric over the more generic click-thru rate because it's a more effective measure of the content of your message. Overall, how can someone click on your message if they never opened it?

Click To Open = (# of unique clicks ÷ # of unique opens) x100

(25 clicks ÷ 50 unique opens) x 100 = 50% CTO

**Unsubscribed:** How many people unsubscribed from your message? (You want this number to be low – if it's high, then you need to change your messaging, style or frequency.)

MailChimp reports the average unsubscribe rate is 0.26%.[xxiii]

**Spam Complaints:** How many people marked your message as spam? (Just like unsubscribes, you want this number to be low. If it's high, then review your frequency and type of messages.)

Remember – you don't need to panic if you have a certain email that gets higher-than-average unsubscribe rates or spam complaints on a specific message, especially if you tested a new format or were selling more than usual. If you see the behavior continue over a couple of email sends, scale back on your frequency or go back to your previous template.

There are a couple of other metrics that you may see:

**Hard Bounces:** Ever get someone's email address wrong and get those return emails that say "This email address doesn't exist"? That's a hard bounce and happens on email lists, too. Your email service provider should automatically remove them from your list.

**Soft Bounces:** A soft bounce is when an email gets to the email server, but then is rejected for another reason. The email address exists, but the email still can't be delivered. This happens often if an email inbox is full, the receiving server is offline, or your email message is too large to be delivered. Most email service providers have a threshold for how many times an email address can "soft bounce" before it's considered a hard bounce and removed from your list.

There are also a few metrics you may want to calculate yourself:

**Conversion Rate:** This is how many people took the action you wanted them to take – not just clicking through on the link, but taking action, like signing up for a free service or event, or making a purchase.

(Number of people who took action ÷ Number of people email was delivered to) x 100
(10 people took action ÷ 150 people the email was delivered to) x 100 = 6.67% conversion rate

**Revenue Per Click or Revenue Per Email:** If you're selling something from your email, you'll want to track how much revenue each email generated. You can do this by using tracking URLs in your message that show up in Google Analytics. (You'll also need to have eCommerce conversion tracking enabled on in your Google Analytics Account.) Some email service providers (like ActiveCampaign) will add the appropriate tracking URLs for Google Analytics, or you can build them yourself using the Campaign URL Builder.

$$\text{Revenue Per Click} = \text{Total Revenue} \div \text{Unique Clicks}$$
$$\$200 \div 25 = \$4/\text{Click}$$
$$\text{Revenue Per Email} = \text{Total Revenue} \div \text{Delivered Emails}$$
$$\$200 \div 150 = \$1.33/\text{Email}$$

**When to Track Email Metrics**

There are two broad types of messages you send as part of your email marketing program: funnels/autoresponders and newsletters. While the statistics you measure on these are the same, the timing of them is different.

**Funnels & Autoresponders:** You'll update the statistics on these on a monthly basis, unless you're running a specific test and need to optimize sooner. If you make any changes to a funnel or auto-responder sequence – like a subject line or an offer – start a new tab on the tracking spreadsheet for the entire funnel.

**Newsletters:** Unlike website metrics, funnels and

autoresponders, you'll want to update your newsletter results each week (assuming you're sending weekly) and for 2 weeks after the newsletter is sent. For example, if you send a newsletter on Monday, September 1, and you update your metrics each Friday, you'll update statistics on that newsletter on Friday the 5th, Friday the 12th, and Friday the 19th (to ensure you've got 2 full weeks of data.) Most engagement will happen within the first 72 hours, but I recommend you report for 2 weeks to ensure you've got those sneaky readers that come back to emails later to read and take action.

Remember, there's a spreadsheet to make it easier for you to calculate all of these metrics on the website.

# Chapter 15
## Amplification Channel Analytics

Each amplification channel will have its own set of available analytics. You'll often have less insight into these channels than your website and email list because you don't own the platform and data. However, still measure your performance on a regular basis to make sure you're getting good results.

### Social Media Channels
Social media is a great tool to learn about your audience through details like audience demographics while also learning what they're interested in. By using a variety of posts in your

social media strategy – not just sharing links to your content – you'll gain valuable insights into what your customers want and need.

Here are the general statistics you'll want to track on a weekly basis:

**Followers:** Since your goal with MVM is support business reach, you'll want to be tracking your follower count over time. If your follower count isn't increasing over time, then you'll need to revise your strategy. Unfortunately, there's no real benchmark for how fast you should grow, as it varies wildly between industries and platforms. Overall, you want to be seeing increases each time you report on the metrics.

**Average Engagement Rate:** The average engagement rate compares your engagement with your overall follower base.

For individual posts, you'll look at:

**Engagement:** Engagement is how much people interact with your content, including likes, shares, and comments. While you'll look at average engagement rates to look at trends, evaluating engagement on individual posts gives you clarity on what types of posts are getting the most attention from your followers.

Beyond just looking at your engagement statistics, you can learn a lot about what your readers respond to so you can create more posts like that.

**Reach:** This metric combines the number of people you've reached both within and outside of your audience. When people engage with your content, their activity is usually shared with their connections, which increases your page's reach.

**Additional Insights from Social Media Metrics Optimal time for engagement:** While you don't need to track each week, you should look at this metric at least once a month to optimize your posting time to reach the most people. Many marketers have their opinions about when the best time to post is – some people say morning, others say afternoons. The fact is that it depends on your audience. The best thing to do when you're getting started is post at several different times, and then use this statistic to find the post times that are best for *your* brand.

**Audience Demographics:** The audience

demographic information that you can get you're your social media followings can be used to refine your ideal customer profile and build paid campaigns. You may also discover that the *wrong* types of people are engaging with your content – so you'll need to change things up! For example, if you run a local gym but you find that most of the people who are engaging with your content are across the country from your location, then you may need to adjust your targeting information.

**Search Platform Metrics**

Search platform metrics are very similar to social media metrics, as you'll be measuring impressions and followers as well as engagement. (Search platforms, discussed in Chapter 8, are sites where you choose to add your content to be found like YouTube and Pinterest.)

**Followers (or Subscribers):** These are the people who not only found your content on your search platform, but also liked it enough that they want to see what new stuff you add.

**Average Impressions (or Views):** Similar to measuring reach in social media channels, page views in website metrics, or opens in email marketing, the average impressions or views measures how often your content is being seen.

**Engagement:** Includes shares/repins and comments. On these platforms, the value of engagement is more important than just knowing that your audience appreciated what you created. Engagement also is a factor in your placement in search rankings: content that drives more engagement also ranks higher in search results. You can encourage engagement by asking your audience questions and responding to comments and feedback.

### Additional Insights from Search Platform Metrics

**Audience Demographics:** Is your content reaching the right people on these search platforms? Or are you reaching a new audience that you hadn't considered? By reviewing your audience demographics on each platform, you'll get additional insights into your potential customers. You may even discover new niches that lead to new marketing campaigns, products, or services.

### Platform Specific Metrics

**YouTube Audience Retention:** After the rise of

DVRs and streaming services, we've all gotten into the habit of binge watching our favorite video series. While Views gives you a strong picture of overall visibility, Audience Retention indicates how long viewers are engaging with your content. You can use this information to ensure your new videos are the right length to maximize viewing – plus you'll see how many people are actually sticking around to hear your call-to-action at the end.

**YouTube Watch Time:** Watch Time measures the estimated total minutes spent viewing your content over time. While Views may seem more important to you, the total time spent on your content more than views is more important to YouTube. Tracking this metric and working to improve it helps you improve your rankings in the YouTube search results.

**YouTube Playback Locations:** Knowing where someone is watching your videos gives you insight into how they found you and what they're doing while they're watching. Some of the common locations include YouTube Channel Page, YouTube Watch Page, Embedded Video, and Mobile Devices.

**YouTube Likes & Dislikes:** While Facebook may not have a thumbs-down button (yet), YouTube does. If your videos are getting a lot of Dislikes, then you may need to review your titles, audience demographics, or production quality. (Of course, you could also be sharing polarizing opinions that not many agree with – which is a brand choice that could lead to these metrics.)

**Pinterest Pins from Your Website:** Many of the standard metrics from Pinterest are about how well you're doing on the platform (and using Pinterest as a tool to drive traffic back to your website). The Pins from Your Website metric gives you insight about how website visitors are sharing your content to Pinterest. If your content isn't getting pinned as often as you'd like, then you may need to test a few different visual styles to improve engagement.

**Pinterest Repins from Your Website:** Repins are included in the overall engagement metric, but they're also important to track individually. A repin is additional evidence about how your visual content is attracting an audience on Pinterest. Repins are the fuel of getting your content in front of new audiences and expanding your reach.

**Advertising Metrics**
You may track the metrics on your advertising even more than you do any of your other amplification channels, simply because every impression and click directly affects your bottom line. Luckily, most of the metrics you'll track in advertising are pretty straightforward.

When you're just getting started, I recommend that you monitor these metrics every week. Once your campaigns are optimized and you're comfortable with your spending levels, you can choose to go down to biweekly or monthly reporting. The most important metric is your cost-per-conversion which tells you how much you're spending to get each customer.

**Impressions:** How many times your ad was viewed. If you're not getting enough impressions on an ad, your targeting may be too narrow.

**Clicks:** How many times your ad was clicked. Clicks indicate how well your target audience is responding to your ad. Too few clicks means that your ad isn't hitting the mark.

**Click-through rate:** Clicks divided by impressions to show you a % of how many people who saw your ad clicked on it.

**Conversions:** How many times your ad clicks resulted in a sale. This could also be conversions to new subscribers or booked calls, depending on the goals of your ad campaign. Your conversions are a measurement of how well your landing page is working – including how well the offer on your ad aligns with the offer on your landing page.

**Conversion Rate:** Ratio of how many people who clicked on your ad converted based on your goal.

**Cost-per-impression:** How much did each 1000 ad impressions cost? CPM helps you improve your targeting by reaching a higher impression count at a lower cost.

**Cost-per-click:** Even if you're buying ads based on impressions, cost-per-click helps you measure how well your creative if is working.

**Cost-per-conversion:** This metric is a holy grail of paid advertising. It tells you how much you spent on each new customer (or subscriber), based on your conversion goal. When you combine your cost-per-conversion with your Customer Lifetime Value, you'll start to truly measure the profitability of ad campaigns to drive new customer acquisition.

**Quality Score or Relevancy:** While the magic mix of factors that goes into quality score or relevancy scores is a bit of a black box, we do know that it includes your past performance of specific campaigns and your account as a whole, the quality of your landing page, and the quality and relevancy of your ad to the target audience. Your Quality Score affects the positioning and importance of your ad. The ad platform, like Google or Facebook, isn't just looking for the highest revenue from each ad it displays – they also want their users to have the best experiences with the ads they see.

Improving your Quality Score can actually improve your performance and get you better results with lower costs. Generally speaking, the higher your Quality Score, the lower your cost per conversion. Remember, a high Quality Score is Google's way of saying that your PPC ad meets your potential customers' needs. The better you are at meeting the prospect's needs, the less

Google will charge you for the ad click.

**Impression Share:** There's a whole world of impressions available – so how many of those impressions are you capturing? By looking at your impression share, you'll know if you're maximizing your reach. Google goes a step beyond showing you the total impression share and also provides insights into if you're losing share based on your budget or your quality score so you know how to improve.

**Return on Ad Spend (ROAS):** Return on Ad Spend is the friendlier version of ROI. To calculate, you simply take the revenue generated from the campaign and divide it by the cost of the campaign. If cost-per-conversion is the holy grail of online advertising than ROAS is the wine. It directly measures how your ad campaigns are affecting your bottom line. It can also uncover some unexpected truths in your advertising. For example, you may discover an ad campaign that has a high cost-per-conversion is also bringing in the most revenue – so it's got a lower ROAS than another campaign that has a lower cost-per-conversion and a smaller average order size.

## Specialized Metrics for Advertising Platforms

**Facebook Cost-Per-Action:** If you're advertising on Facebook then you'll have access to another set of metrics – Cost-Per-Action. Not all ad campaigns come with the same goal (like having a sale), so Cost-Per-Action automatically breaks down your ad campaigns for other goals, including Cost per Page Like or Cost per Comment.

**Frequency:** Advertising on Social Media platforms also gives you insight into frequency or how often someone saw your ad. If you've heard of the Rule of 7 (your prospect needs to hear or see your message at least seven times before they'll buy your product or service), then frequency will make sense. Optimizing frequency is about finding the happy medium between being seen enough that your audience takes action while keeping your ad campaign costs low enough that you can stay profitable.

# ACTION STEPS

Now that we've gone over the metrics you need to track, it's time to start collecting the information. First, go to MinimumViableMarketing.com and download the appropriate tracking spreadsheets.

Then, fill in the historical data so you know where you were before you started implementing an MVM strategy. If you didn't have Google Analytics installed previously, or were not using your selected amplification platforms, that's ok. Your first month of data can act as the benchmark instead.

Next, set a recurring event on your calendar to update your metrics each month. I prefer to do it on the first of each month to see how the previous month did, but if another date range works better for you, that's fine. The important thing is to be *consistent* in how often you're reporting and the date ranges you are reporting on.

# Chapter 16
## Improving Your Results

After you've started tracking your metrics, the next step is figuring out ways to improve them. How do you get more people to click on your "Buy Now" button? How do you get more people to read your blog, follow you on social media, or subscribe to your newsletter list?

There's no single answer that works for every business, every time. There are certainly some best practices that you can follow – many of which I've shared in this book, and will continue to share on the MVM blog. But no one can guarantee that their best practice will work for your business. (If you talk to a marketing consultant or coach that guarantees results, walk away – there are entirely too many variables to guarantee any specific result in a short period of time.)

How you will find out what works for your business is through testing. Using the MVM strategy gives you the gift of being able to test because you're not spinning your wheels trying to keep 15 platforms going. Instead with your highly focused strategy, you can dig into and improve each element of your foundation and amplification efforts.

## How to Create a Good Test
The tests that you'll create for your marketing campaigns are not all that different from the tests you ran in high school science classes. They're just more fun because they affect **your** business – not just trying to create the right hue of blue in the test tube.

## Step 1: Create Your Hypothesis
This is what you think is going to happen – or even the goal of your test. Some example tests are:

- If I increase my Instagram posting frequency

from 3x per week to 7x per week, I will increase my followers.

- I will get higher deliverability if I use a plain-text email format instead of an HTML format.
- I will get more Pins of my blog post if I have a pinnable image above the fold.

Make sure that your hypothesis is something that you have data to benchmark against. You should know how many followers you are getting per week when you've been consistently posting 3 times a week, or what your deliverability is when you've been sending HTML format emails on a regular basis.

## Step 2: Design Your Test
How long do you need to run the test before you'll get results? Usually, you'll need at least 2-3 data points before you can really decide the outcome of your test. During this step, you'll also need to design your test. To create a good test, you should only change ONE thing on each platform at a time. For example, if you're testing the Instagram posting frequency hypothesis, you should continue posting the same types of images with the same hashtags to keep everything as consistent as possible.

For email marketing and paid ads, you may also be able to run a split-test. A split-test is where you have two elements that run simultaneously to the audience to see which gets the best result. Most paid ad campaigns have built-in split testing when you're running several ad variations within a single ad group to see which has better performance.

Email service providers will let you split your list and send two different creatives to two halves of your list. (Each person will only get one email).

**Step 3: Run Your Test**
After you've picked your hypothesis and designed your test, then it's time to put the test into action. If you need to, put a reminder on your monitor or your calendar to not make other changes during the testing period, then do!

**Step 4: Measure Your Results**
Go back to your original hypothesis and your benchmark numbers. Did you see any changes to your metrics? Did they improve, get worse, or stay the same? Were there any other unexpected changes? Sometimes, you'll change something in

one area of your business (like the frequency of Instagram posts), and you'll see results somewhere else (like getting more email subscribers).

## Testing versus Strategic Decisions

While I'm an advocate for testing in your business, sometimes you'll just need to make a strategic decision about something. For example, one client I was working with wanted to test an affiliate program to expand the reach of her online course. When we were talking through the set-up and offer, she kept referring to it as a test.

I asked, "Are you going to shut down the affiliate program if it doesn't do what you expect?"

Of course she wasn't. It was too much work to set up the affiliate program and recruit affiliates just to shut it down in a few weeks or months.

Starting an affiliate program wasn't a test – it was a strategic decision for her business.

Maybe creating unique graphics every week for your HTML email campaigns takes too much time, so you decide to go to a standard branded header. That's a strategic decision. You don't need to run a test to decide.

How do you know when something is a strategic decision or if it needs a test?

- Is it something that requires a large commitment of time, money, or resources? If so, then it's a strategic decision. If you're feeling unsure about making a commitment to the decision, then break it down. What is the next best step you can take that moves you in that direction?
- If you know you want to do it – no matter what the outcome – then it's a strategic decision for your business. As the boss of your business, you have the right to make those decisions. You also need to own the consequences of those decisions – good or bad.
- If it's something that you're curious about – either because you've seen someone else doing it, or you've dreamed up something totally new – then it's a test.

Here are a few examples of tests I've run with my clients and in my own business:

- Highly designed emails (a lot of graphics) vs simple design (mostly text)
- Email send days and times
- Subject lines and ad headlines
- Button colors – on landing pages, websites, and in email campaigns
- Bing vs Google Adwords (run the same ad on both platforms to see which has better performance)
- Resource Library vs eCourse Lead Magnets

•

# PART 5
## Finding Success With Minimal Viable Marketing

Success with MVM goes beyond just finding the right platforms and getting the right metrics. Now that you understand the MVM system, it's time to establish your goals, increase your productivity, and manage your time efficiently.

# Chapter 17
Goal Setting

As a business leader, goal setting is not a new
concept. But if you're not establishing and going
after the right goals, your business may be
suffering for it. Let's take a quick look at why
goals are important - not just for having a
destination, but also for building and maintaining
motivation.

Goal setting as a tool for motivation is actually a
relatively new concept. In the 1960s, Edwin Locke
shared his goal-setting theory of motivation,
stating that specific and challenging goals along
with appropriate feedback contribute to higher

and better task performance.

Of course, if we look at this realistically, people have been setting goals for hundreds of years – just without the same performance measurements. Stockpiling enough firewood to get through the winter was more about survival than mere task performance. Since survival has gotten easier, we need different kinds of goals. And according to Locke, those goals must have **specificity, commitment, challenge,** and **feedback.**

Taking that a step farther George T. Doran introduced S.M.A.R.T. goals as a tool to create criteria to help improve the chances of succeeding in accomplishing a goal in 1981.

The acronym stands for:

S – Specific
M – Measurable
A – Achievable
R – Relevant
T – Timebound

There are hundreds of resources available that go into greater detail on SMART goal setting, from planners to apps to accountability communities. I

share a few of my favorites over on
minimumviablemarketing.com

In the meantime, here are 9 tips to creating goals
for business (and yourself!):

1. **Break it down.** Most business planning is
   done for the year, which is too large to take
   action on easily. As Brian P. Moran points out
   in *The 12 Week Year*, most teams accomplish
   more in the last few weeks of the quarter and
   the fourth quarter of the year because they're
   operating under time constraints to
   accomplish those goals. By breaking down
   your larger goals into smaller goals, you'll
   build momentum and a sense of
   accomplishment.

2. **Measure your progress.** Of course, this means
   that your goals will need to be measurable. (It's
   the M in SMART goals, after all!) Knowing
   your progress toward your goals will be
   measured provides an incentive to accomplish
   those goals. You can also create micro-goals to
   ensure you're on track. For example, if you
   have a goal to release 2 new podcast episodes
   per week, and it's Thursday night and you

haven't released any, you probably will not meet your goal of two episodes per week.

3. **Commit to your goals.** Don't just skim this one and move on, thinking it doesn't apply to you. We've all set goals – often in the form of New Year's Resolutions – that sound good on paper, but don't mean much to us in the long run. We don't commit to the goal, so we don't get out of bed to go for those early morning runs. Choose goals that are important to the success of your business, and truly commit to them. MVM helps with this by providing you a strategic focus for your marketing efforts.

4. **Leverage a support system.** We are more likely to accomplish goals that we have committed to publicly. If you're in a business with multiple people, then you may use your team as part of the support system to keep it on track. If you're a solopreneur, coach or consultant, then you may be part of an in-person or online business network that gives you accountability. This support system provides you with a necessary feedback loop to keep you moving forward. (If you're looking for this kind of network, then join the MVM network at minimumviablemarketing.com/community)

5.  **Stay flexible.** Listen, life happens. Sometimes a client project will need to take center stage and will push your goals a little off track. Other times, it may be your daughter's dance recital. Staying agile allows you take advantage of opportunities while maintaining your cool.

6.  **Accept imperfections.** Even the best sports players miss sometimes. They don't shoot 100%. Great directors and actors have films that flop. World class writers have typos in books. To be successful, you have to let go of your perception that everything needs to be perfect. In fact, perfect is the enemy of the good *and the finished.*

7.  **Don't stop moving.** When you realize you're not going to reach a goal, it can stop you dead in your tracks. Even when your progress seems minimal, the only way you'll accomplish your objectives is step-by-step. As long as you continue moving, you're continuing on the path to success.

8.  **Think positively.** In the same way that missing a goal may cause you to pause in your

tracks, it can also affect your thinking and mindset. Focusing on the lessons you've learned from your experiences and using those to think positively about your future outcomes helps you achieve both short- and long-term success.

9. **Celebrate success.** Speaking of success, don't forget to celebrate your successes regularly. Even if you didn't hit your goal of growing sales 20%, celebrate your 15% growth. Did you get twice as many people to attend your webinar as you planned? A celebration is definitely in order.

**Types of Marketing Goals**
Now that you know more about goal setting in general, it's time to dive into what types of marketing goals you should set for your business. Marketing goals should be specifically related to improving your visibility and reach to new and existing customers. Some common goals that related to marketing include:

- **List growth:** This is the number of new people who join your email list. List size over time is an important metric because the people on your email list will be one of your warmest audiences for offers. They've given you the keys to their email castle. It is a top-of-funnel activity that signals awareness and interest.

- **Lead generation:** Lead generation takes list growth a step farther – moving a subscriber from interest to evaluation using discovery calls and other micro-commitments. (Remember, every action, engagement, page view, retweet, and download are micro-commitments that help move prospects into customers.) Not all leads will come through this pathway – some may find you and immediately move to a demo or sales call.
- **Sales:** In direct sales organizations or eCommerce businesses, sales are also a function of how well marketing is doing.

If you're comparing goals with others, you may also see that they set goals around activities like page views, social media engagement or social media followers. Remember that these softer metrics are valuable for measuring brand awareness, but overall they may have little impact on the success of your business. Your competitor's 10,000 Instagram followers don't mean much if they never buy – whereas your 1000 raving fans can sell out a new launch in minutes.

# Chapter 18
## Getting It All Done

So far, we've been talking a lot about the things you'll be doing to establish your Foundation and pick your Amplification platforms. Even with an MVM strategy, all those activities can expand to take up your whole day (or week) if you let them. That's why creating marketing calendars and processes that work for your working style is an important component of MVM. Grab your pen and paper (or spreadsheet) and let's start getting all these goals broken down into plans and – most importantly – actions.

**Marketing Calendars**

Your marketing calendar is a key foundation for getting everything done. It's where you plan your campaigns and special offers, allowing you to categorize and prioritize your activities. They also allow you to spot "bunches" in your marketing activity when you're running too many offers and campaigns simultaneously. (You'll also see holes where you don't have enough going on!)

## JANUARY

| Sunday | Monday | Tuesday | Wednesday | Thursday | Friday | Saturday |
|---|---|---|---|---|---|---|
|  |  | **1** Sale Your New You Sale / Mastermind Call / Blog Post Launch | **2** Facebook Promo | **3** Instagram Promo / Podcast + interviews | **4** Twitter Promo / Podcast + interviews | **5** Instagram Live |
| **6** | **7** Book Sale (Jan 7-30) / Facebook Live / Podcast | **8** Book Sale (Jan 7-30) / Mastermind Call / Blog Post Launch | **9** Book Sale (Jan 7-30) / Facebook Promo | **10** Book Sale (Jan 7-30) / Instagram Promo / Blog Post Launch | **11** Book Sale (Jan 7-30) / Twitter Promo / Podcast + interviews | **12** Book Sale (Jan 7-30) / Instagram Live |
| **13** Book Sale (Jan 7-30) | **14** Book Sale (Jan 7-30) / Facebook Live / Podcast | **15** Book Sale (Jan 7-30) / Mastermind Call / Affiliate Promo 1 / Blog Post Launch | **16** Book Sale (Jan 7-30) / Facebook Promo / Affiliate Promo 1 | **17** Book Sale (Jan 7-30) / Instagram Promo / Affiliate Promo 1 / Podcast + interviews | **18** Book Sale (Jan 7-30) / Twitter Promo / Affiliate Promo 1 | **19** Book Sale (Jan 7-30) / Instagram Live / Affiliate Promo 1 |
| **20** Book Sale (Jan 7-30) / Affiliate Promo 1 | **21** Book Sale (Jan 7-30) / Facebook Live / Affiliate Promo 2 / Podcast | **22** Book Sale (Jan 7-30) / Mastermind Call / Affiliate Promo 2 / Blog Post Launch | **23** Book Sale (Jan 7-30) / Facebook Promo / Affiliate Promo 2 | **24** Book Sale (Jan 7-30) / Instagram Promo / Affiliate Promo 2 / Podcast + interviews | **25** Book Sale (Jan 7-30) / Twitter Promo / Affiliate Promo 2 | **26** Book Sale (Jan 7-30) / Instagram Live / Affiliate Promo 2 |
| **27** Book Sale (Jan 7-30) | **28** Book Sale (Jan 7-30) / Facebook Live / Podcast | **29** Book Sale (Jan 7-30) / Mastermind Call / Blog Post Launch | **30** Book Sale (Jan 7-30) / Facebook Promo | **31** Book Sale (Jan 7-30) / Instagram Promo / Blog Post Launch |  |  |
|  | **Notes:** |  |  |  |  |  |

Most marketing calendars have multiple tiers to accommodate deeper levels of detail.

### Tier 1: Master Schedule

Your master schedule is where you plan major campaign launch dates, including sales and special offers. Depending on your business model, you may create an annual master schedule, or plan quarter by quarter. Using the start and end dates of these campaigns and launches, you'll create your individual tactic calendars, including content calendars (for blogging, videos, and podcasts), email calendars, and social media calendars.

**Tier 2: Tactic Calendars**
Your tactic calendars break down the individual activities that you'll be taking on a weekly or daily basis for each of your tactics. Many entrepreneurs make the mistake of documenting launch dates for tactics, without calculating and planning for the time needed to actually create those tactics. Some of the things you'll include in your tactic calendar include:

- Email newsletter sends
- Social media posts
- Special offer launch dates (including ad campaign start and end dates)
- Press release launch dates
- Announcements (like if you're being featured on a podcast or in the press)
- Special dates for your industry (tax deadlines for accountants, sprinkler system maintenance for landscapers, holiday shipping deadlines for

## Tools to Create Marketing Calendars

There are dozens of ways to create marketing calendars. The easiest and most accessible is a simple spreadsheet with a single tab for your master schedule, and a tab for planning each tactic. If you're following the MVM framework, your calendar will have the following 5 tabs:

- Master Schedule
- Content Calendar
- Email Calendar
- Amplification Channel 1
- Amplification Channel 2

*A sample spreadsheet template is available in the MVM Resource Library.*

You can also build your marketing calendar in Trello using boards:

- Board 1: Master Schedule
- Board 2: Content Calendar
- Board 3: Email Calendar
- Board 4: Amplification Channel 1
- Board 5: Amplification Channel 2

*Grab the link to sample Trello boards in the Resource Library!*

Whatever format you choose, your marketing calendar needs to include the following information:

- Campaign start and end dates
- Campaign goals. Whether it's increasing your email list size, generating additional leads, or driving sales, you'll want to have SMART goals to measure your success. On your calendar, it's important to remind yourself of the goal of each campaign so your messaging aligns and you're launching campaigns to support all of your major goals for the quarter or year.
- Messaging notes: If you have initial thoughts on the messaging, like seasonality, include those in your master schedule.
- Links to any supporting documentation and collateral. By adding the links to (or locations of) your documentation and collateral, you'll save yourself a lot of time later.

**Task Lists & Project Management**
Once you know what you need to do, then you'll need to organize how you're going to get it all done. This is where task lists and project

management tools become important. Before you pick a solution, you'll need to answer 2 questions:

1.  *Are you doing all your own marketing (including graphic design) or are you working with a team (virtual or otherwise)?* If you're working independently, you'll have more choices in project and task management solutions, because you won't need to share visibility with others. It's hard to share a bullet journal or paper planner with a virtual assistant working halfway around the world.

2.  *What's your organization and accountability style?* Without going into project management methodologies, you'll want to figure out which system works best for you to help you find the right systems to keep you on track. Some people can get along with a spreadsheet. Others need a lot of reminders and rewards.

If you're envisioning your desk as a pile of papers and sticky notes on every visible surface, and reminders on your calendar and in the notes app on your phone and think you don't have an organizational style… that's not really true. You just may not have found one that works for you yet.

In order to make the most of your MVM strategy, you need to find the one that's going to work best for you. Here are some of the most popular project and task management methods and systems:

- **Spreadsheets.** Spreadsheets are incredibly versatile tools that allow you to create almost any type of project management system you want. You can build links between tabs or even separate workbooks, create automations with macros, use color coding and more. But unfortunately for some, a spreadsheet won't send you a reminder message the day you need to start writing that blog post.
- **Asana**. Asana is task-based project management. Projects have sections, tasks, and subtasks. It's well designed to work with teams, as each task (and even subtask) can have a team member assigned along with a due date. You can also collaborate using comments, keeping your project work out of email. You can turn on notifications and use the Asana mobile app to keep you on track with your task due dates. Tasks are either finished or unfinished – there are no

additional statuses available, although you can use sub-tasks to track the progress of a single task.

- **Trello**. Trello is also a project and collaboration tool with many features similar to Asana, including collaboration, task management, and subtasks. Unlike Asana where tasks are either complete or incomplete, in Trello you can have any number of statuses in the form of columns. Tasks are "cards" within those columns or lists. Trello uses visualizations to allow you to drag cards into different lists based on their statuses. Lists don't have to just be statuses - they can be anything you want. That's why in the Trello Inspiration library you'll find templates for everything from wedding planning to organizing kids artwork to pizza places in each of the 5 New York City boroughs.
- **Whiteboard**. A whiteboard is hard to take with you in your pocket for productivity on the go, but it can give you a lot of real estate for planning and some visual reminders of your goals and tasks.
- **Paper and pen.** Whether you purchase a pre-printed paper planner or create your own with a blank notebook (like a bullet

journal), paper and pen have the advantage of being available anytime – whether you're on a bus, train or plane, or at your desk. You don't need internet connectivity to capture an idea or mark something as complete. Of course, it also won't send you reminders and it's one of the hardest to share with a team for collaboration.

I use a combination of Asana and spreadsheets for most of my project and task management, along with a whiteboard for brainstorming and outlining new processes and marketing campaign flows. It turns out my brain really loves to work in bulleted lists with sub-bulleted lists. Many of my more creative clients, particularly graphic designers, artists and writers, prefer the more free-flowing nature of Trello.

## Creating Processes

You'll also need to understand the steps you need to take to implement each of your campaigns and tactics. By understanding (and documenting) your marketing processes, you'll reduce the amount of time you spend on tasks and improve your overall quality. Plus, your stress levels will go down because you won't be forgetting steps or scrambling to get it all done. And when the time is right to expand your team, either with virtual assistants or on-site employees, you'll be ready to hand over the reins.

The first step in creating a process is identifying the trigger that causes the process to start. This can be an activity or state within your business. A few examples could be:

- 90 days before new product release
- 45 days before the sale begins
- Fewer than 10 blog posts in the queue
- Less than 2 weeks of social media scheduled

Then, figure out the major steps that need to happen after the trigger. The bigger the process, the more major steps there will be. Include the end of the process and what you'll have when it's over.

Your document will probably look a lot like this right now:

Process Name: Sale Prep

| Trigger | Step 1 | Step 2 | Step 3 | Step 4 | Step 5 | END |
|---------|--------|--------|--------|--------|--------|-----|
| 45 days before the sale begins | Define sale offers & products | Graphics | Prep Store | Emails | Social Media | All marketing collateral is created and scheduled |

As the proverb says, the devil is in the details, and it's no different in documenting your marketing processes. You'll need to go 1-2 steps deeper to really have a good template for this process. As we follow through the eCommerce store sale prep process, we'll go one layer deeper. You could go another level on each of the steps to provide more detail on what it takes to create the graphics, prep the store, create the emails, and the social media posts. They could also be related sub-processes that run within the larger process as a whole since this sale isn't the only time you do some of those activities.

If at this point you're thinking, "Man, what about documenting processes is minimum *or* marketing?" Marketing is hard work – even with MVM in your back pocket. Creating processes for your most common marketing activities makes it easier. When you have a process to follow you don't have to do a rush job on your campaign like slapping default fonts on stock photography to create blog post graphics.

After you've finished documenting the process, you'll need to test it. The best way to any process is to follow it the next time you're running that marketing project within your business. Make updates based on the activities that you forgot, or that need to be done in a different order. You may end up doing this several times before your processes run like well-oiled machines.

If you're already working with a team, make sure to add who is responsible for each step of the process. It's also helpful to document what software you use for each step.

Process Name: Sale Prep

| Trigger | Step 1 | Step 2 | Step 3 | Step 4 | Step 5 | END |
|---|---|---|---|---|---|---|
| 45 days before the sale begins | Define sale offers & products | Graphics | Prep Store | Emails | Social Media | All marketing collateral is created and scheduled |
| Substeps | [ ] Review results of the last sale<br>[ ] Decide on offer<br>[ ] Verify inventory availability (if selling a physical product) | [ ] Shop Graphics<br>[ ] Website ads<br>[ ] Social Media Graphics<br>[ ] Email Graphics | [ ] Set up coupon codes<br>[ ] Test coupon codes<br>[ ] Create any needed landing pages<br>[ ] Schedule graphics | [ ] Create messages<br>[ ] Add Graphics<br>[ ] Test messages<br>[ ] Schedule for sending | [ ] Create messages<br>[ ] Add Graphics<br>[ ] Schedule for posting | |
| Responsible Party | Brandi | Sarah | Brandi | Brandi | Brandi | |
| Software/ Systems | N/A | Photoshop, Canva | Shopify | ActiveCampaign | Hootsuite, TailWind | |

## Using Processes

When you've ironed out the processes, it can help to add them to your project management system for easy reference and future use. Depending on how often you're using it, you can either create a template (that you then copy each time you're running the process) or create a single project that you reset and reuse.

Asana and Trello are two of the most popular digital task management systems that you can use to track and re-create these processes as well as your projects.

## Optimizing Processes

The more you use a process, the more you should look for ways to optimize those processes. That may include using more templates and automations, including tools like Zapier that help integrate your systems and minimize your manual effort.

**Eliminating steps.** Each step in your process needs to add value to the overall goal. If you identify any steps that are not adding value but are taking time, eliminate them.

**Automation.** If you're doing something a robot

could do, then automation may be a good solution. For example, you can use email service providers like ActiveCampaign and ConvertKit to send a specific email series after someone makes a purchase from your site. If you find you spend a lot of time going back-and-forth to schedule meetings, Calendly or Acuity can allow your customers to schedule their own appointments (in blocks that you set).

**Delegation.** There comes a time in your business when it makes more sense for someone else to handle part of your work. It may still need to be done by a human, but that doesn't mean that you have to be the one to do it. Many business owners employ virtual assistants for even a few hours a month to handle some of those tasks. This may include social media management, creating transcriptions from podcasts for blog posts, or packing and shipping orders.

For example, one of my clients wanted to optimize their podcast creation process. Their initial process was taking over 3 hours to produce after they finished recording. First, they found some steps that they could eliminate – like trying to edit out every filler word or pause in the episode. They also decided to create a few stock promotions for their products that they can edit into episodes, rather than always recording a new promotion. They also started using a transcription service to save time (and money) on their VA. Finally, they signed up for a podcast distribution service to increase their reach and saving time.

Now that you've got your plans laid out in a marketing calendar, figured out how you're going to manage your projects, and identified your processes, let's take a look at how to manage your time to get the most done.

## Time Management Techniques

Parkinson's law states: *"Work expands so as to fill the time available for its completion."* This is true for everything – whether it's fun (like a dinner party with your closest friends) or drudgery (like trimming the hedges). That's why it's important to use effective time management techniques to get the most done in the least amount of time. By limiting the amount of time you have to work on something, it forces your brain to focus and get more done. Here are some techniques that time management experts swear by.

**Pomodoro Technique.**[xxiv] With this technique, you

work in "Pomodoros" – 25 minutes with short breaks in between. (It was named after the tomato-shaped kitchen timer known as a Pomodoro timer.) The original technique has six steps:

1.  Decide on the task to be done.
2.  Set the Pomodoro timer (traditionally up to 25 minutes).
3.  Work on the task.
4.  End work when the timer rings and put a checkmark on a piece of paper.
5.  If you have fewer than four checkmarks, take a short break of 3-5 minutes, then go back to step 2.
6.  After four Pomodoros, take a longer break (15-30 minutes), reset your checkmark count to zero, and start over at step 1.

The goal of the Pomodoro technique is to reduce the impact of internal and external interruptions on focus and follow. During a Pomodoro, you will need to turn off all notifications (that includes your phone and email!). The strictest rules state that if you get off-task during a Pomodoro, you don't earn the checkmark and you have to start over.

There are many ways that this technique has been adapted for the modern entrepreneur. I've known some people who do double duty with their Pomodoros and HIIT workouts - work for 25 minutes, work out for 5. I use the concept of a Pomodoro to manage social media. Three times a day, for up to 25 minutes each time, I engage on social media. It keeps me off social for the rest of the day - and to be honest, sometimes it's hard to get to that 25-minute mark!

**Batching.** Doing a series of similar work can make it easier to get more done in a shorter amount of time. Shifting between tasks or attempting to multitask can reduce your productivity by up to 40%[xxv]. When you batch tasks, you focus on just one set of related tasks for a period of time, allowing your brain to focus more deeply, call on more creativity, and get more done.

To start, group tasks logically by their function – like social media scheduling or writing. You can also create 'theme days' where you focus on one type of work for the entire day.

| Monday | Writing (blogs, newsletters, social media posts) |
|--------|--------------------------------------------------|
| Tuesday | Business development (cold calls, networking) |
| Wednesday | Graphic design (social media posts, blog graphics, video thumbnails) |
| Thursday | Social media (schedule social media for all amplification platforms) |
| Friday | Learning (read blog posts and books, watch videos and webinars) |

These theme days don't have to last the whole day. After all, if you're implementing a MVM strategy, the goal is to NOT spend all day on your marketing. Batching and theme days can still improve your productivity in the limited amount of time that you're allocating to your marketing.

**Scheduling.** There are certain times of the day that you're just firing on all cylinders and things seem easier. You can do more, better work during your peak hours.

For most people, peak alertness starts a few hours after you get to work – around 11 am, and starts to decline at 3 pm. There is a second peak at approximately 6 pm. For maximum effectiveness, schedule your highest value work near one of these peak times. Then use those lower-energy windows to do the lower-value activities, like scheduling appointments.

**Delegation.** Of course, one of the biggest ways to get more done is to have help doing it. One of my favorite sayings to deconstruct is "You have the same number of hours in a week as Beyoncé – no excuses!" The fact is, we all do have the same 168 hours per week to wash our hair, brush our teeth, spend time with our children – and, oh yeah – make a living. It's a fine comparison to make when you also consider that Beyoncé and her husband Jay Z have as many as 100 employees to help them manage it all. If each of those employees is working 40 hours a week, that's an additional 4000 hours of time dedicated to keeping their household and businesses running.

Certainly, we all can't afford to hire like them. But for your business to grow over the long term, you may need to hire some help for either low-value tasks or activities that are outside of your realm of expertise, so you're less efficient. Some common things for business owners to outsource include social media management, graphic design, bookkeeping, and customer service.

**Two-Minute Rule:** David Allen, author of *Getting*

*Things Done* introduced the two-part 2-minute rule.

- Part 1: If it takes less than 2 minutes, just do it. Don't add it to your to-do list, put it aside for later, or delegate to someone else. Just do it.
- Part 2: If it takes more than two minutes, start it. Once you start acting on small tasks, you can keep the ball rolling. Simply working on it for two minutes will help you break the first barrier of procrastination.

These time management techniques get even more powerful when you combine them. You can batch tasks into your Pomodoro windows to double-up on productivity. Then schedule those Pomodoros during your peak productivity times. Test them and determine which are best for you.

For instance, I love using batching and Pomodoros together. I can sit down in one Pomodoro and outline several podcast episodes. Then, in the next couple of Pomodoros, I record my episodes and get them ready to schedule. Finally, I can take my notes and turn them into blog posts, and create the graphics. It may take me 6-8 Pomodoro sessions to get 4 podcast episodes ready along with their associated blog posts and promotional graphics, but that also means in less than 4 working hours, I have created a month's worth of content.

Sometimes I know I need to get started on a project but it seems a bit overwhelming (or I'm just not in the mood). That's when I break out the Two-Minute rule. Usually I don't even notice when the two minutes is up because I'm already deep into the project.

# TIME TRACKING CHALLENGE

This won't just help you manage the way you're spending your time on marketing your business; it will help you uncover other opportunities to increase efficiency throughout your business. You may discover things you can outsource and things you can stop doing completely.

I've used this exercise extensively when training new marketers and when coaching overwhelmed business owners. Most of them fought it - and believe me, I get it. It's annoying. It's boring. It feels like you're already out of control of your time, and now I'm asking you to spend your time tracking your time.

For one full week, document what you're doing every 30-minutes. It may seem tedious or like overkill, but this is how you're really going to understand where your time goes. Don't try to shortcut the system either – you're only going to get the improved clarity when you take the exercise seriously. If you do this once a quarter, you're tracking your time for less than 8% of the year.

## How to Do Your Time Tracking Challenge

Download the time tracking challenge template from MinimumViableMarketing.com.

Print out the time tracking challenge template and keep it next to you all day. Every 30 minutes, take 30 seconds (or less) and jot down what you've spent the last period of time doing. (Yes, this may distract you from your tasks, but it's well worth it to understand where your time is going. Plus, with the 30-minute windows, you can easily get a Pomodoro block within each slot.)

Don't limit your tracking to work time. Also track how long you're sleeping, how much time you're spending with family and friends, exercising, watching TV, learning, or anything else you do!

After the week is over (all seven days), then analyze where your time has gone. You can start by breaking them down into personal and business. Then take it a step further into more descriptive categories. For personal categories, it may be things like self-care, family time, and hobbies. Within your business, you'll have administrative duties (like answering email or checking the mail), marketing activities, sales activities, finance, and more.

Were you surprised at where your time went? I'm surprised every time I do this to see how much time I spend on activities I find hard to categorize.

Now that you know where your time is going, you can start to make changes. You can create a schedule for yourself based on how much time you need to do certain things, and how much time you WANT to spend on others (like recreation or family time).

# Chapter 19
## Overcoming Procrastination

Now that you've set goals and have some tips on how to get organized and manage your time to get everything done, it's time to tackle the biggest mindset challenge in marketing your business: Procrastination.

We've all procrastinated from time to time - whether it was doing the laundry or writing a term paper. When we procrastinate in our business, the ramifications are much larger than having to wear a suit to work or pulling an all-nighter to finish the paper. Procrastination can have long-term negative effects on your business progress *and* your self-esteem.

There are four main causes of procrastination:

1. **A fear of failure.** Unconscious procrastination is comforting when you fear failure. Your brains use the logic "You can't fail what you don't try." Of course, failure is not fatal in most circumstances. If you try something and fail, you have the opportunity to learn from that failure and learn from those mistakes. If you never try, you also miss those opportunities to learn.
2. **Excessive Perfectionism.** If your expectations are much higher than what you can reasonably accomplish, you're less likely to start until you believe you can do it perfectly. You worry that you can't meet your own high standards. It's amazing how many "imperfections" that we as consumers don't even notice, or if we do, they just make the creator human.
3. **Low energy levels.** Too little sleep, unhealthy diets, and high levels of stress all can contribute to feeling like you just can't get off the couch and take action. Increasing your self-care and balance in your lifestyle can help you

overcome the procrastination that comes with low energy.

4. **A lack of focus.** This is one of the biggest procrastination causes that MVM tackles. A lack of focus may appear as being overwhelmed – because you don't know what to do next, so you do nothing. Well defined goals and a clear, simple strategy help give you the focus you need to decide what action to take next.

*We don't get overwhelmed when we have too many things to do. We get overwhelmed when we don't know what to do **next**."* – Unknown

Just as there are tools to help you manage your time better, there are models to help you overcome procrastination due to lack of focus.

**Eisenhower Matrix**

The first and most popular tool to help you overcome procrastination helps you identify and do the most important work. Created by Dwight D. Eisenhower, 34th President of the United States, the Eisenhower Matrix has been used for decades to help leaders make the most of their time.

It's easy to get caught up in the Urgent but Not

Important, or the Not Urgent and Not Important because they're often perceived as EASIER than the truly important work.

|  | Urgent | Not Urgent |
|---|---|---|
| Important | **Do it now**<br>- Write an article for today<br>- Deadline driven projects<br>- Pressing Clients | **Schedule: Decide when to do it**<br>- Exercising<br>- Calling family & friends<br>- Researching articles<br>- Long-term business strategy |
| Not Important | **Delegate – who can do it now?**<br>- Booking a trip<br>- Scheduling interviews<br>- Approving comments<br>- Answering certain emails | **Delete: Purge task**<br>- Obsessively checking social media<br>- Working on a dead project |

## Eating the Big Frog

This one comes from beloved American author Mark Twain:

*"If it's your job to eat a frog, it's best to do it first thing in the morning. And If it's your job to eat two frogs, it's best to eat the biggest one first."*

Rather than making this about having frogs for breakfast, it's about prioritizing the biggest, most important activities first. Just as the Eisenhower Matrix gives us a framework for deciding what is truly urgent and important for our business, the

concept of eating the big frog adds another layer –
anticipation. There are things in our businesses
that are both urgent and important – that we
**dread.** Maybe it's replying to a particularly
challenging client, or creating the outline for a
webinar. And when we dread something, we put
it off. (If you don't believe me, ask your dentist's
office how many reschedule calls they get a day!)

Why is it important to do dreaded, urgent, and
important tasks first? Well, beyond getting them
out of the way, you'll also be able to approach the
rest your day with a sense of accomplishment.
After you've marked that big ugly frog off your to-
do list, the rest of your list will seem like a breeze.

Here are some frogs just waiting to be eaten:

- Sending off a proposal to a new client
- Making 5 cold calls (for sales or networking)
- Scheduling the date of an upcoming
  webinar
- Promoting a new product
- Applying to be a speaker at an industry
  conference

**Eating an Elephant**
While we're on the eating metaphors, let's also
tackle "How Do You Eat an Elephant?"

The answer: "One bite at a time."

Joking aside, we also procrastinate when activities are too big. For example, if your to-do list is "Build the website," and you've never built a website before, you're probably going to put it off because it's too big and too overwhelming. To eat that elephant, break it down into smaller pieces. Before you build a website, you'll need a domain name and hosting. Then you'll need to pick a content management system.

Here are some tasty elephants you may be facing:

- Creating a course
- Writing a book
- Running your first PPC ad campaign
- Creating a Facebook Group
- Building an automated sales funnel

In the MVM Resource Library, you'll find several template checklists for common marketing activities that you can use as a starting point to break down those elephants into bite-sized chunks.

**Five Second Rule**

The last procrastination tip to share is from *The Five Second Rule* by Mel Robbins. This procrastination rule doesn't revolve around eating, but it sounds like it could. Robbins points out that procrastination isn't related to being lazy or unmotivated. Procrastination is a behavior designed to help us avoid stress. Whatever we're procrastinating from doing is stressing us. The longer we put it off, the longer we're putting off the stress.

So how does the Five Second Rule overcome this? It uses neuroscience to get your thinking prefrontal cortex out of the way so that you can move forward before your back is against the wall. The Five-Second rule has two simple steps:

1.  Acknowledge that you're stressed. You don't need to analyze or dissect why you're stressed, just know that you are.
2.  Make a five-second decision that is directly contrary to the stress response. Robbins calls this a *decision of courage*. Maybe it's picking up the phone to make that phone call to schedule an appointment or writing for just 5 minutes. The key is to actually TAKE the action, not just decide what the action should be and then

spend hours analyzing the decision or planning to take the action.

According to Robbins:

*"There is a window that exists between the moment you have an instinct to change and your mind killing it. It's a 5-second window. And it exists for everyone. If you do not take action on your instinct to change, you will stay stagnant. You will not change."*

**Putting it All Together**

Now that we've gone over several different techniques for getting it all done – whether it's about managing your schedule or overcoming procrastination, it's time to put it to work. As Mel Robbins would say:

*"If you don't physically move within 5 seconds, your mind WILL kill your dreams."*

So get moving. Try out these techniques and see which works best for you. You can use them individually or combine them. Some days you'll need to count down the 5-second-rule to get yourself moving. Other days you'll eat the big frog with relish and have an amazingly productive day. There will be ebbs and flows.

But armed with your MVM plan and these productivity and proactivity techniques under your belt, you'll be able to get more done and get better results in a fraction of the time.

# PART 6
Beyond MVM

# Chapter 20
## The Next 90 Days And Beyond

Maybe this last chapter seems strange if you love the principles of MVM. There's really no reason that you can't maintain momentum by optimizing your MVM channels.

But chances are – at some point in your marketing journey – you're going to want to expand your channels. Some shiny object will be irresistible. You'll want to spread your wings and test something new to see how it does.

Maybe one of your amplification channels won't work as well. It may lose traction in the market, start charging more than you're willing to pay, or even go out of business completely.

What do you do then?

## Adding Amplification Channels

When you're considering adding another amplification channel, start with the review process that we did when choosing the original amplification channels in Chapter 7.

As a quick refresher, you'll want to understand:

- Market reach
- Ideal frequency
- Time investment to create needed messaging
- Competition involvement
- Financial investment needed

Remember, the Amplification Channel Review worksheet is part of the Resource Library, available free at MiniumumViableMarketing.com

Once you've identified that you do want to add the channel, start with a 60-90-day test of the new platform. During this test, measure engagement, audience growth, and conversions.

If your test does not meet your benchmark goals, review your strategy and test a different strategy or close the platform.

If the test meets or exceeds your benchmark goals, then decide if you're adding the channel to your existing marketing strategy or replacing an under-performing channel.

### Handling Under-Performing Channels

Sometimes what's always worked on a platform stops working. Maybe it's because the audience needs and interests have shifted like the growth of live video in 2017 and 2018. Other times, the platform itself has changed, like when Facebook changed their algorithm in January 2018 to prioritize personal pages and groups over Business pages. Or, you may have also reached a saturation point with your market.

All of these changes are inevitable. In fact, what was working 6 weeks ago may not work now. By tracking your platform engagement regularly on the MVM Tracking Dashboard, you should see these trends very quickly, giving you the opportunity to pivot.

When you see a change starting, head to the source to see if something on the platform has changed. Quick searches for key terms like "[Amplification platform] update [Current month & year]" (i.e., "Facebook update August 2018") will quickly uncover any news about the algorithm or other platform changes that have been reported or noted by leading sites.

If there are platform changes, typically one of the major marketing news sources will have a wealth of information about the changes and what we need to do as marketers to adapt to the change. (Check out the Resource Guide for some of my favorite sites.) For example, when Facebook updated their algorithm to prioritize personal pages and groups, many marketers created their own groups, or started investing in Facebook ads and boosted posts to maintain their reach. After a few weeks, marketers also learned how to get more organic engagement on their posts through live videos and creating more conversation on their pages (rather than just doing one-direction "push" style posts). Some have actually seen reach increase since they've implemented these new strategies.

If no platform changes have been announced, then

it's time to do a deep-dive evaluation of your efforts over the last 30-45 days. Look at each effort and ensure that you've done the same level of effort to share. Everyone is guilty of going through low-effort periods, and this would be reflected in your metrics.

In this deep-dive evaluation, look at the views and engagement on all of your shared effort:

- How many times were your ads or posts seen?
- How many clicks did they drive to your site?
- How many likes, comments or shares did it generate?
- What trends can you identify?

Next, look at your aspirational users and competitors. Are they using any new techniques that you're not? While you won't be able to see all of their metrics, social media is very transparent about many of these metrics, including likes, comments, and shares.

Between your deep-dive evaluation and the review of your aspirational (competitors) and active competitors, you'll uncover trends of what's working that you can start moving into your mix. Identify 1-3 new tactics you'd like to incorporate. Some things you may consider include:

- Sharing more audio or video content
- Leveraging more user-generated content
- Testing new messaging on an ad
- Asking more questions to drive engagement
- Change your visual messaging from photos to illustrations (or vice versa)

Start leveraging these new tactics in the next week or two. Leveraging the MVM method of scheduling no more than 30 days in advance, you should be able to easily add these new tactics to your promotional mix.

Remember to measure frequently during the test period to see if your new tactics are moving the needle. During a test, I measure results every 3 days rather than waiting for the weekly review. (I'm also known to be a bit impatient when it comes to seeing results.

## Shutting Down Low-Performers
There are times when no amount of re-strategizing will "save" a platform. Maybe the demographics are wrong for your customers, or your place in the

market has changed. Sometimes the platform itself changes so much that it no longer makes sense for the way you want to engage with your customers. If you've already tried the strategies to handle an under-performing channel, and it hasn't made a difference in at least 30 days, then you may need to consider shutting down the platform instead of continuing to invest your time.

In these cases, you'll need to plan a graceful exit. Depending on the platform, you have several choices to close down your presence.

For platforms that don't have a time-based news flow, you can quietly stop posting. This is ideal for platforms like Pinterest where your content can continue to live on without someone noticing that you haven't updated the account in weeks or months.

For newsfeed and time-stamped platforms, like most social media including Facebook, Twitter, and Instagram, create a "See You Soon" style post. Be sure to include a call to action to join your email list and follow you on another platform where you will be posting regular updates. Be sure to pin this post to the top of your profile, so when someone visits they're not surprised that the last update was weeks or months ago.

Finally, for community-driven platforms, including Facebook or LinkedIn Groups or Slack communities, you'll want to give your community plenty of notice about the upcoming closure. Be clear with them about why you're choosing to close the community – and where they can continue to engage with you. If your community has also been providing customer service support, be sure to give them access to other channels to gain the support they've come to depend on.

# CONCLUSION

Congratulations! If you've been working through this book with me, then you've established your MVM strategy. You've got a great website to send new and existing customers to, you've built a great email list to stay in touch with prospects and customers alike, and you've picked two amplification channels to spread your offers far and wide. Plus, you've got strategies under your belt to make the most of your limited time. And you know what to do when you're ready to expand, or something isn't going the way you want.

This book is just the beginning of the MVM

journey. If you haven't already, be sure to visit the companion website at MinimumViableMarketing.com for updates, worksheets, and more.

For more help:

## Course
Are you more of a hands-on learner? Then the MVM course may be right for you!

- Follow along with video lessons and worksheets
- Get feedback on your specific business questions.
- Community of like-minded business owners to share experiences
- Updated lessons on new amplification platforms and new strategies

Learn more:
MinimumViableMarketing.com/Course

## Coaching
Want to work with me one-on-one?

- Personalized feedback on your specific marketing strategies – from brand through execution

- Monthly metrics review
- Accountability to stay on-track (including my techniques to combat "shiny-object" syndrome)
- Available on a quarterly basis.

Learn more:
MinimumViableMarketing.com/Coaching

**Community**
I want to hear about your experiences with MVM!
Drop me a line anytime -
brandi@minimumviablemarketing.com

**If you found this book helpful, please leave a review on Amazon!**

# ACKNOWLEDGEMENTS

There are two people without whose help and support this book could not have been written: my mom – who has always believed in me unconditionally and fully; and my husband who not only read every word, talked me through every revision, and changed countless diapers so I could write, re-write, pull my hair out, and write some more.

I also wish to extend my heartfelt thanks to the following people for their generous assistance: my pre-release readers, including Sarah Guilliot, Natasha Scott, and Nic Widhalm, whose feedback helped make this book infinitely better; and my clients over the years who have allowed me to learn with them and develop this framework.

# About The Author

Brandi C. Johnson is a marketing consultant and coach for small business owners and entrepreneurs. After spending 15 years in corporate marketing, she shifted her focus and expertise to help business owners build and implement their own marketing strategies – without having to become marketers themselves. She has a Bachelor of Science in Business Administration with emphasis in Marketing, and a Bachelor of Arts in Technical Journalism from Colorado State University. She also has additional graduate-level coursework in marketing, project management, and business administration.